D1300271

In this exciting collection of monologues, the authors expand the voices of biblical women and, in so doing, find a way to speak things that are regularly deemed unspeakable in Judeo-Christian tradition: they graphically describe their experiences of sexuality, embodiment, and trauma; they remember and resist religion's collusion with women's submission, suffering, and silencing; and they express their religiosity comingled with anger, longing, and fraught relationships. This is certainly a book that would make Eve Ensler proud.

KRISTI UPSON-SAIA

Associate Professor of Religious Studies, Occidental College

Lady Parts

Lady Parts

Biblical Women and *The Vagina Monologues*

Edited by Kathryn D. Blanchard
and Jane S. Webster

WIPF & STOCK · Eugene, Oregon

LADY PARTS
Biblical Women and *The Vagina Monologues*

Wipf & Stock
An imprint of Wipf and Stock Publishers
199 W. 8th Ave., Suite 3
Eugene, OR 97401
www.wipfandstock.com

ISBN 13: 978-1-62032-311-3

MANUFACTURED IN THE U.S.A

CONTENTS

Contents

List of Contributors

Jo-Ann Badley is Professor of New Testament at the Seattle School of Theology and Psychology.

Jessica Becker Beamer is a speech language pathologist living near Detroit, Michigan.

Kathryn D. Blanchard is Associate Professor of Religious Studies at Alma College in Alma, Michigan.

Meredith Brown is a graduate of Alma College, where she majored in religious studies.

De'Anna Daniels is a student at Union Theological Seminary in Richmond, Virginia. She is a graduate of Alma College, where she majored in religious studies.

Crystal Davis is a student at Barton College, where she majors in nursing.

Emily Havelka is a graduate of Alma College, where she majored in English.

Lisa Nichols Hickman is a Presbyterian pastor and author of *The Worshiping Life*. She is currently a PhD candidate in theology at Duquesne University in Pittsburgh, Pennsylvania.

Mallory Magelli is a graduate of Barton College, where she majored in religion and philosophy. She is currently a seminary student at Vanderbilt University in Nashville, Tennessee.

Celecia Manning is a student at Barton College, where she majors in religion and philosophy and biology.

Jessica Paige is a graduate of Alma College, where she majored in women's and gender studies.

Cate Pugliese is an elementary school counselor living in the Pacific Northwest.

Jamie A. Smith is an independent scholar of European Renaissance history and resides in Maine.

Dolly Van Fossan is a graduate of Alma College, where she majored in sociology and minored in religious studies.

Lizy Velazquez is a graduate of Barton College, where she majored in social work. She is currently a social worker in Wilson, North Carolina.

Maggie Watters is a graduate of Alma College, where she majored in psychology and religious studies.

Jane S. Webster is Professor of Religious Studies at Barton College in Wilson, North Carolina.

INTRODUCTION

Biblical Midrash and *The Vagina Monologues*: Strange Bedfellows?

Kathryn D. Blanchard and Jane S. Webster

IF YOU HAVE SEEN fit to pick up a book with a name like *Lady Parts: Biblical Women and* The Vagina Monologues, it probably means you do not need to be persuaded that the Bible is alive and well in the twenty-first century. You may also not need much convincing that it is worth the time and energy of both Christians and Jews—clergy, scholars, and laypersons alike—to keep the biblical texts alive by cultivating contemporary interpretations. Moreover, you may agree that at least some of those contemporary interpretations should make women and girls the primary interlocutors.

What may surprise you, however, is that this particular project involves rewriting parts of the Bible using Eve Ensler's play, *The Vagina Monologues*, as a main source of inspiration. Since its first performance in the 1990s, the monologues have been performed on more than a thousand college campuses each year and have spawned imitators such as *The Penis Monologues: Men Speak*, *The Naked I*, and *The Queer Bathroom Monologues*.

They have caused a great deal of controversy and consternation around the globe, especially among religious folks, due mainly to the graphic language concerning women's sexuality and genitalia that is embedded in their first-person narratives. Such exposure is anathema in certain circles of orthodox religion (though not all). Nevertheless, we find Ensler's play to be an ideal diving board for women's biblical exegesis about women, precisely because of its shock value; it refuses to leave women in silence, even when their stories are unpleasant or heterodox. We therefore invite readers to approach this volume with compassion, not only for the biblical women whose stories are rife with suffering, but also for the contemporary authors who are working out their own theologies through first-person storytelling.

Though this particular pairing of vaginas with the Bible is unconventional, the broader desire to "uncover" women in Scripture is not at all a new project. Since at least as far back as Elizabeth Cady Stanton's *Woman's Bible* (1898), many generations of readers have drawn attention to the fact that most women in the Bible are invisible, unless they are in some way furthering the plot of one of God's chosen men—usually in the role of wife, mother, prostitute, or victim, though occasionally also in a more active role like midwife, warrior, or even assassin.

A quick search of Amazon.com (or even the tiniest college library collection) reveals dozens of volumes from the 1980s and later about women in the Bible. Among these are several collections of first-person narratives, many of which seek to give voices to characters in the Bible who have traditionally been overlooked or oversimplified. Despite their worthy task, however, some of these available collections may be difficult for certain contemporary audiences to relate to, steeped as we now are in postmodern skepticism and third wave (or possibly even fourth wave) feminism. Such earnest utterances as, "The Lord has blessed me with a desire to really know the women of the Bible,"[1] or "What

---

1. Roseanne Gartner, *Meet Bathsheba: Dramatic Portraits of Biblical Women* (Valley Forge, PA: Judson, 2000), vii.

wealth of spiritual courage these women show. What instinctive understanding of the divine in their lives. Thanks be to God for them,"[2] certainly have the power to draw in some readers; but they may alienate others for whom the language of evangelical Christianity is non-native. There is still room in the conversation for interpretations of biblical women's stories that speak more pointedly to the alienation that many women—not only atheists and agnostics, but even many devout Jews and Christians—feel when they encounter the Bible and its offspring.

Those of us who teach religious or biblical studies are keenly aware of this kind of alienation. Female students, in particular, often express shock, disgust, and anger upon reading prominent biblical stories in which female characters are raped, murdered, bereft of their children, prostituted, or cast aside for a more fertile wife. Such stories, moreover, since they are told from male characters' points of view, usually appear with little or no commentary from the narrators to indicate that such treatment of women might be unacceptable in Jewish or Christian life. These stories raise questions for many women that deserve to be asked out loud. As Carol Christ wrote in 1978, "Biblical tradition warrants the view that humans have a right and even a responsibility to question God, to wrestle with God, until the answers to human questions are revealed."[3]

Thus arose the pedagogical idea to invite students to read biblical stories about women, informed by feminist exegesis, through the lens of *The Vagina Monologues*. The task of the exercise was to help students understand what one Hebrew Bible scholar calls engaging "the social and conceptual worlds of the ancients without normalizing [i.e., giving authority to] their understandings of sexuality and sexual expression in ways that

2. Katerina Katsarka Whitley, *Speaking for Ourselves: Voices of Biblical Women* (Harrisburg, PA: Morehouse, 1998), 8.

3. Carol P. Christ, "Expressing Anger at God," in *Women's Studies in Religion: A Multicultural Reader* (Kate Bagley and Kathleen McIntosh, editors; Upper Saddle River, NJ: Pearson/Prentice Hall, 2007) [originally *Anima* 5.1 (1978)], 105.

ignore violence against women."[4] Students did research and scholarly exegesis about biblical texts that included female characters, after which each student wrote a monologue in the voice of a character she selected. But more than merely "giving voice" to these biblical women, students also gave special attention to fleshly experiences; instead of merely naming women's emotions, they also dared to name women's embodiment, both on the page and in live readings. From these efforts to perform incarnations of lost or hidden biblical women, this volume was born.

As for our book's title, it was difficult to come up with something that might make reference to *The Vagina Monologues* while remaining "appropriate" for theological audiences—suggestive, but not outright offensive. In the spring of 2012, as we were considering the particular euphemism we eventually settled upon, a *Non Sequitur* comic strip appeared that seemed to confirm our choice.[5] In it, a group of men sit in a diner drinking coffee. A waitress asks them, "So what're you boys up to this mahnin'?" They tell her that they've noticed that all the world's troubles are "intah-connected" and must thus be traced to a single cause. "So what'd you boys decide is the source of all the problems in the wahld?" she asks. One man answers simply, "Lady pahts." The idea is funny only because we recognize a kernel of tragic truth in the fact that men have traditionally blamed their problems on women (think Helen of Troy, or Yoko Ono). Likewise, one of the Bible's tragic truths is that women and girls are often blamed, justifiably or not, for the problems men suffer in the text, beginning famously, of course, with Eve. The cartoon was a kind of sign for us that we had stumbled upon the right title. So we decided on *Lady Parts*: performable dramatic "parts" about women's private parts.

4. Sandie Gravett, "Reading 'Rape' in the Hebrew Bible: A Consideration of Language," *Journal for the Study of the Old Testament* 28/3 (2004) 290, explanation added.

5. Wiley Miller, *Non Sequitur* (April 8, 2012). www.gocomics.com/nonsequitur/2012/04/08.

Having described the genesis of this somewhat unorthodox project, the remainder of our introduction will address three important tasks. First, we will locate our work within the long tradition of biblical midrash, as well as the younger tradition of feminist midrash. We will then explain more fully why we believe *The Vagina Monologues*, because of their global appeal and despite (or because of) their controversial language and substance, constitute a uniquely appropriate model for women's exegesis in the early twenty-first century. Finally, we will offer a brief description of the monologues that follow, and offer some thoughts on how to read them. We thereby hope to convince even skeptical audiences that such a project is, at the very least, justified by interpretive tradition, even if it is not likely to reshape the Judeo-Christian world overnight.

Midrash, Biblical Exegesis, and Women in the Bible

As we have suggested, this project draws on both traditional and contemporary interpretive practices rather than being entirely innovative. Retelling biblical stories has roots deep in Jewish tradition, even as deep as the Bible itself. Take but one example: 1–2 Samuel and 1–2 Kings describe the turbulent years of Israel's history from the prophets' perspectives, laying the blame for the Babylonian exile at the feet of the kings who worshiped other gods. 1–2 Chronicles, meanwhile, retell these same stories from the priests' perspectives, adding details about temple practice that the prophetic narratives ignored. This process of retelling continued in early Jewish *midrash*, a term drawn from the Hebrew letters *Da-Re-Sh* ("search") that reflects an effort to understand through the act of interpretation or *exegesis* (literally, "drawing meaning out of the text").

One important collection of midrashim (plural of midrash) is called Midrash Rabbah, which contains verse-by-verse interpretations of the Torah and the Five Scrolls (Ruth, Esther, Lamentations, Song of Songs, and Ecclesiastes), the biblical books read in Jewish liturgy. These interpretations were composed by Jewish rabbis over several hundred years and eventually gathered into collections. Traditionally, there are two types of midrash. The first, *midrash halakhah*, analyzes the law with logic or deductive reasoning, comparison, interpretation through the lens of another biblical text, or with exposition by example or story. The second genre, *midrash aggadah*, explains or elaborates biblical stories with the addition of new details or by juxtaposition to other stories. The important balance of law and story reflects something we all know intuitively from our own learning as children. A parental law such as "Look both ways before you cross the street" might be clear enough, but is more persuasive when followed by a story: "That little boy in a wheel chair once ran out into the street without looking and was hit by a car."

Law and storytelling persuade in their own ways; the same type of dialogue between story and law is found in the biblical text itself. For example, the law in Deuteronomy 25:5–6 states that when a man dies without an heir, his wife is to be given to her brother-in-law to bear a child for her husband. Genesis 38 reiterates and fleshes out this idea in telling the story of Tamar, a woman who was denied her promise of a child by her father-in-law, and who finds justice for herself through seduction. The law and the story are in conversation with each other, explaining, reinforcing, challenging, and—in some cases—softening with mercy. Thus, the rough spots and contradictions in biblical texts have traditionally been viewed as God-given opportunities to challenge the interpreter to fill them in, to make sense of them.[6] Ancient scholars were writing *with* Scripture, as Jacob Neusner describes it, not *about* Scripture.[7] In other words, the intent of midrash was not to limit or close the meaning of the Scriptures once and for all, but rather to construct and articulate faith as an

6. Reuven Hammer, *The Classic Midrash: Tannaitic Commentaries on the Bible* (New York, NY: Paulist, 1995), 31.

7. Jacob Neusner, *The Midrash: An Introduction* (Northvale, NJ: Jason Aronson, 1990), x.

ongoing process. Midrash allows readers to think through the Scriptures again and again in new contexts.

This traditional Jewish approach can stand in stark contrast with the habits of some modern Christian exegetes, who often attempt to find the "real" or the "closest historical" meaning of a particular biblical idea, in order to establish an unquestionable and eternal interpretation.[8] Where the Jewish tradition generally prefers to hold meaning open, the recent Christian tradition has been more comfortable when meaning is closed. (Think, "God said it; I believe it; that settles it.") It is beyond the scope of this project to provide a thorough history of Christian biblical canon but, to oversimplify somewhat, the desire to close the meanings of Scripture can be traced to the reformations of sixteenth-century Europe. In order to challenge the ultimate authority of the church's hierarchical tradition, Martin Luther and other Protestant reformers sought a new, more impartial authority: the Bible. In place of popes and bishops, Protestants claimed the Bible as the sole revelation of God, and argued that everything necessary for salvation could be found therein, with no need to appeal to human tradition. Indeed, while the Catholics had claimed that "outside the church there is no salvation" (*extra ecclesiam nulla salus*), the Protestants retorted that "only Scripture" (*sola scriptura*) held the keys to salvation.[9]

This change in doctrine accompanied radical changes in Christians' access to the Bible. Up until then, the fourth-century Latin Vulgate had provided a single text to unite all of Christendom—at least for the very few people who could read Latin and

8. See for example, James L. Kugel, *The Bible as It Was* (Boston, MA: Harvard University Press, 1997).

9. While the rhetoric of Protestant reformers often centered on the idea of *sola scriptura* as the source of Christian authority, they nevertheless drew widely from Catholic tradition (especially St. Augustine) in order to make their theological arguments. They also maintained church structures that included ordained clergy; the major difference was that clergy would now have to appeal to Scripture, rather than tradition, to justify their pastoral teachings and practices.

had access to a Bible. In the early modern period, the Vulgate was gradually set aside in favor of new translations in the spoken languages of the people, such as German and French; and with widespread use of the printing press (invented in the 1400s), these vernacular Bibles and theological tracts could be produced more and more cheaply. The Bible thus became ever more available to the laity, and sixteenth-century Christian individuals and communities began to read and interpret the Bible for themselves in unprecedented ways.

As a challenge to the Catholic Church, this new emphasis on Scripture was effective. But perhaps somewhat ironically, it was also effective in preventing a monolithic "Lutheran" or "Calvinist" church from taking over in Rome's place. While reformers might have liked to be able to determine the one true meaning of Scripture for all Christians in all times and places, Scripture's meaning could not be pinned down after it had been set loose. Once churches were untethered from centuries of Roman rule, multiple Protestant denominations were inevitably born, each based on its own particular interpretation of Scripture. This great pressure on the Bible continued into the early modern era as the only authoritative locus of divine revelation for Protestants (although personal revelation would later give it a run for its money), necessitating that each new group of Protestants identify and clarify their "best" translation and interpretation.

In the last century, particularly in the United States, the Bible has taken on even more authority for some people in response to various factors. As international travel and immigration have increased, so has exposure to people of other faiths and cultures. Some Christians have found it necessary to defend their faith politically and socially, and have resorted to taking adamant stands on particular doctrines or statements of faith using the Bible as their ultimate authority. Since, for example, the question of same-sex marriage has become a matter of considerable public debate, some Christians have used biblical passages such as Leviticus 18:22 and Romans 1:26–27 that renounce same-sex relations, in order to justify their claim that marriage (despite a rather inconsistent biblical witness on the subject[10]) is exclusively between one man and one woman. Others use the creation accounts in Genesis 1–2 to stand up against scientific accounts of the Big Bang theory or Darwinian evolution; still others point to the story of Noah to insist that global warming cannot be taking place because God said the earth would never again be flooded (Genesis 9:11). To question the standard interpretation of the biblical text is, for some contemporary Christians, to question the trustworthiness of salvation itself.

But there has never been a standard interpretation for all Christians. Closing the meaning of the Bible—that is, determining the "best interpretation" once and for all—has its problems, as anyone who has read the Bible with attention can attest. Those who see the Bible as the inerrant word of God, literally true and historically accurate, must go to significant lengths to explain its inconsistencies, contradictions, and difficult passages. For example, if we compare the presentation of women in the letters of Paul, we would note that in some letters Paul seems to affirm the equality of women (Galatians 3:28), and he even promotes Phoebe as a leader of the church of Cenchreae (Romans 16:1), while in other epistles Paul instructs women to be silent in church (1 Timothy 2:12) and obedient to their husbands (Ephesians 5:22). If meaning is closed, then Paul must mean one thing or another, but not both. Some would then make a chronological argument that the later texts must be given priority over the earlier, for Paul corrected himself: women *used to* be permitted to talk but should now be silent. Others would argue that Paul was never actually affirming women in leadership roles in Romans 16, but simply mentioned them in passing; this particular reference therefore carries no authoritative weight. Still others argue

10. Examples of the Bible's mixed comments about marriage include Abraham, who used his wife's slave to have a child; David, the "man after God's own heart" (1 Sam 13:14), who had multiple wives (2 Sam 2:2; 12:24; 1 Kgs 1:2); Jesus, who renounces his own family of origin (e.g., Matt 12:47–49; Mark 10:29); and Paul, who urges celibacy for Christians instead of marriage (1 Cor 7:7–8).

that his commands in Timothy or Ephesians were meant only for their particular congregations, rather than as a general rule for all Christians.

Another way of dealing with scriptural self-contradiction is by controlling the translation. Some English-speaking readers, for example, promote the exclusive use of the King James Version of the Bible, first published in the 1600s. The KJV preserves the masculine "kinsman" to refer to the apostle Junia (a female's name), under the assumption that women cannot be apostles (Romans 16:7). The KJV also hides more recent scholarly observations that suggest, for example, based on the style of the original Greek and the flow of the argument, that the strong prohibition against women speaking in church in Paul's first letter to the Corinthians (14:34–36) was inserted by a later hand to correct Paul's open attitude to women in leadership. Such choices in translation and interpretation attempt to eliminate the contradictions found in the New Testament texts about the role of women in the earliest Christian churches. To leave the contradictions visible and the meaning open would make room for the possibility that women may have been actively engaged in the formation, leadership, and promulgation of the early churches, even if those roles might have changed over time and from place to place. To leave this meaning open would, by extension, open the possibility for women to play greater roles in church leadership today.

Closing the meaning of the Bible has become a more acute problem in the last several decades as women around the world have been exploring and advancing their roles in the public domain, including participation in the religious lives of their communities. This has been made possible in part through their advanced education in biblical studies and theology. But to search the biblical texts for explicitly celebrated models of women who were active outside of the domestic realm is to search with frustration. Those few biblical women who have stepped out of their homes have usually done so as a last resort, when their men have failed in some way. In the Hebrew Bible, for example, Deborah leads the Israelites into battle when their general, Barak, lacks the courage (Judges 4–5). In the deuterocanonical books, Judith goes out to defeat the Assyrians when the male elders of her town want to surrender (Judith 10:9–10). Indeed, for a biblical woman to step outside of her house is often to risk her very life, as when Jephthah's daughter leaves the house and her father offers her to God as a burnt sacrifice (Judges 11:30–40). In the New Testament, Paul's first letter to Timothy instructs him to prohibit widows from "gadding about from house to house" (5:13). Again and again, the Bible is disappointingly clear: Christian women—like all Greco-Roman women in late antiquity—do not legitimately belong in the public sphere. The matter, it seems, is closed.

What are Jewish and Christian women to do in light of the ambivalence that Scripture expresses toward them? Those who are troubled by the authority of the Bible because it does not apparently promote women's equality have typically responded in three main ways: "to remain silent, to leave, or to confront."[11] Some rationalize the authority and submit without question; such people may not necessarily be satisfied with what they read, but may despair of having other faithful options. Others reject the Bible's authority outright and separate themselves from church or synagogue altogether, dubious that genuine reform of patriarchal tradition is possible.[12] But some critics choose to struggle with the nature of the biblical text and its authority, and remain part of their religious communities with the hope that the church or synagogue can ultimately be reformed from within.[13] In order for this last group of readers to make sense of the authority, then, they have to find new ways to read the Scriptures.

In her seminal work on the subject, Elisabeth Schüssler Fiorenza challenges the closure of biblical meaning, and proposes

11. Christ, "Expressing Anger at God," 102.

12. Most famously, see Mary Daly, "'The Women's Movement: An Exodus Community,'" *Religious Education* 67 (1972) 327–333.

13. Sarah Hearner Lancaster, *Women and the Authority of Scripture: A Narrative Approach* (Harrisburg, PA: Trinity, 2002), 1.

that women read both the biblical text *and* its interpreters with a feminist hermeneutic (or interpretive lens), which includes four main "moments."[14] In the first moment, she encourages women to read with *suspicion*, aware that the Bible has an androcentric (male-centered) perspective and promotes patriarchy (father-rule). It was written for men, by men, and about men; the lives of women lie on the margins of that story. This original marginalization of women is then exacerbated by mistranslation of pronouns in the biblical text: when Greek and Hebrew refer to a mixed group of people, both male and female, these languages use the generic plural masculine pronoun. In other words, "they" looks masculine grammatically but could refer to a collection of both men and women—or even a group predominantly of women. In a similar way, all of humanity has previously been called "mankind," referred to generically as "all men," even when the presence of women is implied.[15] "Such language," says Schüssler Fiorenza, "not only makes women marginal but also makes them invisible in the written classics of our culture, among which the Bible is preeminent."[16] In recent years, English speakers have begun to adopt more inclusive language; this is also true of biblical translations where the text is ambiguous about the gender of the participants. For example, the New Revised Standard Version, first published in 1989, replaces "men" with "people," "brothers"

---

14. See, in particular, *In Memory of Her: A Feminist Theological Reconstruction of Christian Origins* (New York, NY: Crossroad, 1992). These steps are outlined by Elisabeth Schüssler Fiorenza in *Bread Not Stone: The Challenge of Feminist Biblical Interpretation* (Boston, MA: Beacon Press, 1984), 15–22. Modifications are noted in "Feminist Hermeneutics," pages 783–791 in volume II of *The Anchor Bible Dictionary* (New York, NY: Doubleday, 1992).

15. It was authors Casey Miller and Kate Swift who first brought wide attention to the problematic nature of masculine language in English in "Desexing the Language," *MS Magazine*, December 1971. They later expanded their argument in *Words and Women* (New York, NY: Doubleday, 1976) and *The Handbook of Nonsexist Writing: For Writers, Editors, and Speakers* (Bloomington, IN: iUniverse, 2001 [1980]).

16. Schüssler Fiorenza, *Bread Not Stone*, 17.

with "brothers and sisters," and "the man who" with "the one who," in an attempt to render women more visible in the text.

In the second moment, Schüssler Fiorenza encourages women to read the Bible with a hermeneutic of *resistance*: to "read against the grain," actually rejecting the androcentric bias and authority found in the text. When we read with resistance, she says, we challenge the objective and assumed authority of the text as self-sustaining and self-generated; this involves her controversial assumption that the Bible is not necessarily revelatory, despite traditional claims made to that effect. So, for example, when a twenty-first-century woman reads the description of "the good wife" in Proverbs 31:10–31, she might appreciate that this is what a first-millenial B.C.E. Judean man—or his mother, but *not* necessarily God—would want his wife to be like. Schüssler Fiorenza thus calls contemporary women to resist the androcentric, patriarchal bias of the text they have inherited.

In the third moment, she encourages *remembrance* of these texts in order to preserve those "dangerous memories." Even if biblical texts are not revelatory, she claims, readers can still accept the Scriptures as evidence that there "once was a time" when it was socially acceptable for men to offer up their wives for rape, to send them into the desert, or to bring other women into the family to bear their children. If women were to discard these stories or stop reading them altogether, they might be lulled into thinking that those sorts of things could never happen. As much as women may abhor these stories, they must not forget them. They are the only biblical heritage available to Christians and Jews who wish to remain in their religious traditions and change them, rather than abandon them.

The final moment, according to Schüssler Fiorenza, is to critically *reconstruct* the history of women using the remnants of evidence found in the cracks of men's history. This final move is a necessary step, for if Christian and Jewish women cease to ground themselves in the text, they relinquish their biblical heritage and lose the promise of its liberation. She therefore encourages women to re-create and celebrate the arising vision of the woman who is liberated from the text through creative acts of liturgy, drama, dance, poetry, and art. She urges all Christians—both male and female—to view the biblical text not as an archetype that aims to set an eternal standard for human social life, but as a prototype, the "first try" at articulating religious understanding that will only improve with age and extensive tinkering.[17] The biblical text must thus remain open to new meaning in order to accommodate the challenges of growing awareness and understanding. This brings us back to midrash, one of the traditional ways to tinker with this reclaimed image of women in the biblical text.

Where the Jewish sages kept the biblical text open with midrash, our project attempts to keep the meaning of midrash itself open. Whereas traditional midrash teaches, questions, and explores the meaning of the biblical text, contemporary midrash has become an exercise for—and in some cases enactment of—theological reflection. So rather than be limited to the traditions of the past and the constraints of authority, more and more people, including women, are exploring the edges of the production of midrash, taking greater interpretive risks than have ever been taken before. Even then, however, many fear to tread in areas that might undermine the authority of the text, the social construct of gender inherent in the text, and/or perhaps most importantly the authority, benevolence, and justice of God.

Nevertheless, some interpreters in recent decades have pushed the edges of their own courage to ask the more difficult questions, such as: What if we stand in the shoes of "the other" and experience this story from their perspective? If we take the perspective of the Canaanite inhabitants of Jericho, for instance, Joshua's conquest of the land becomes a cruel and vicious genocide (see Joshua 6). Another approach is to challenge the assumed righteousness of the biblical characters; for example, reading "against" the figure of Abraham, the story of Hagar and

17. Ibid., 61.

Ishmael might become a story of domestic abuse and violence. In a charming but disturbing collection of "counter tales," Norma Gangel Rosen retells the story of Abraham's attempt to sacrifice his son Isaac, first from the terrified perspective of Sarah as she watches from a distance, and then from the point of view of Rebekah, who must deal with a husband always looking over his shoulder for the father who tried to kill both his sons.[18]

Yet another midrashic approach is to attempt to flesh out a story by filling in the bare-bones biblical narrative with interesting details that enliven the story and contribute an additional layer of meaning, or what some call "discursive elements." In other words, the way a story is told can communicate as much as, if not more than, the story itself.[19] So, for example, Lois T. Henderson tells a novel-length romance about Lydia the dyer of purple; drawing on very limited biblical details (Acts 16), she presents Lydia as a woman who needs and wants a man to take care of her.[20] In a later novel about Priscilla, the wife of Aquila,[21] Henderson promotes Priscilla's independence and leadership role in her community. With these two novels, Henderson allegorically reflects the transition of women's roles in the contemporary church, while locating the "authority" of her stories firmly in the biblical text. Similarly, in the best-selling phenomenon *The Red Tent*, Anita Diamant recaptures and reframes the story of Dinah

18. Norma Gangel Rosen, *Biblical Women Unbound: Counter Tales* (Philadelphia, PA: Jewish Publication Society, 1996).

19. Katerina Katsarka Whitley, *Speaking for Ourselves: Voices of Biblical Women* (Harrisburg, PA: Morehouse, 1988), tells women's stories from their perspective but preserves the patriarchal biases of the text, promoting the dominant and central role of men. Jill Hammer, *Sisters at Sinai: New Tales of Biblical Women* (Philadelphia, PA: Jewish Publication Society, 2001) (re)captures the richly spiritual, poetic, and artistic lives of women in the Bible, opening space for women's religious experience.

20. Lois T. Henderson, *Lydia: A Novel* (San Francisco, CA: Harper and Row, 1979).

21. See Acts 18:2, 18–27; Romans 16:3; 1 Corinthians 16:19; 2 Timothy 4:19. Lois T. Henderson with Harold Ivan Smith, *Priscilla and Aquila: A Novel* (San Francisco, CA: Harper and Row, 1985).

and the women who support her (Genesis 34), while leaving her famous father and twelve brothers in the margins.

In *I Am . . . : Biblical Women Tell Their Own Stories*, Athalya Brenner, a leading feminist biblical scholar, retells women's stories not to recapture the intention of the original authors (though this is still a legitimate academic pursuit in some circles) but rather to express her own concerns in a hybrid style that combines academic discourse with popular imagination. Specifically, she selects women from the text whose deaths have not been described; informed by the biblical text, cultural history, and Jewish rabbinic midrash, semantics, and philology, she allows them to live on and "speak today." In the voice of Zillah, for example (Genesis 4), she says, "we get to have stories imagined after our names. And we have supplemented the story here—without dwelling too much on our husband's history, since the sages do it extensively without our aid."[22]

The "Lady Parts" in this book thus belong within the rich and growing context of biblical interpretation, reading with suspicion, resistance, and remembrance. While the language in some of these monologues may be more risqué than most readers are conditioned to expect, while these monologues do not shy away from naming female bodily experiences such as rape and miscarriage, and while some of the monologues dare to depart from the "facts" of canonical texts (would Lilith have it any other way?), we are nevertheless participating in the ongoing practice of reading, understanding, and questioning Scripture. In doing so, this volume holds nothing to be off limits, but draws on an alternative locus of the sacred: the embodied experiences of women, in the inevitably varied forms they take. Our hope is to open the biblical texts, to read them in new ways, to become more aware of the complex relationships of power and gender that existed then and exist now, and thus to promote a dominant ethic of compassionate listening.

22. Athalya Brenner, *I Am . . . : Biblical Women Tell Their Own Stories* (Minneapolis, MN: Fortress, 2005), 23–24.

Why *The Vagina Monologues*?

Because the word "vagina" has the uncanny power to offend so many listeners—especially those with religious sensibilities—Eve Ensler's *The Vagina Monologues* is not the most obvious pairing for biblical exegesis.[23] Nevertheless, we believe this particular text has the potential to produce rich conversations about women and Jewish and Christian Scripture among twenty-first-century students, clergy, and scholarly experts alike. As interpreters seek to relate biblical stories to their own lives—sometimes by direct application, by exploiting silences in the text, or by rejecting explicit meanings in favor of creative alternatives—their diverse results belie the idea that there is one fixed meaning of Scripture for all times and places. *The Vagina Monologues*, likewise, questions the "closed meaning" of the vagina, whether as a sacred inner sanctum, a devil's gateway, a portal to mysticism, a birthing canal, or a morally neutral piece of anatomy. Eve Ensler's play calls audiences to a particular way of reading the world that pays special attention to the fates of global women at the turn of the twenty-first century. In particular, it calls attention not only to women's social, cultural, or political roles but especially to their *embodied* experiences—specifically the experiences in and around their vaginas.

This has not always been an easy sell. When Eve Ensler first wrote and performed the monologues as a one-woman show in

23. It seems, however, that the word "vagina" may now be going mainstream. During this writing, for example, congressional leaders are debating the virtues and vices of transvaginal ultrasounds (Kate Shepherd, "Mandatory Transvaginal Ultrasounds: Coming Soon to a State Near You," *Mother Jones*, March 5, 2012; www.motherjones.com/mojo/2012/03/transvaginal-ultrasounds-coming-soon-state-near-you); network television is throwing the term into more and more of its prime time shows (Mary Elizabeth Williams, "Television's Season of the Vagina," *Salon*, September 26, 2011, www.salon.com/2011/09/26/vagina_sitcom_season). More recently, a Michigan state congresswoman was censured for using the word "vagina" in a speech on the floor of congress; #ladyparts has been trending on Twitter; and Naomi Wolf has created a media stir by publishing *Vagina: A New Biography* (New York: Ecco, 2012).

the late 1990s, she admitted to having intense fears about how it would be received. "You feel guilty and wrong [when you say 'vagina']," she wrote, "as if someone's going to strike you down."[24] The play had arisen almost accidentally as an outgrowth of her own attempts to heal from childhood rape, a process that had included interviewing more than two hundred women about their vaginas. Having realized the deep qualms she herself had about uttering the name of that body part, so vulnerable to abuse, she got up the courage not only to say the word out loud, but even to ask her interviewees the jarring question, "If your vagina could talk, what would it say?" This almost shockingly simple (some would say juvenile) act of saying "vagina" was hugely instrumental in empowering her and her conversation partners to move beyond shame and trauma, or even just the day-to-day indignities of their female bodies. Over time, she scripted a number of monologues based on these interviews and set out to perform them.

She did not predict the variety of responses she eventually got. After letting taboo lips speak, she was soon overwhelmed by countless women from her audiences who came to share with her, to speak their own unspeakable vaginal experiences, to thank her for helping them finally name their own pain and suffering. This outpouring of traumatic stories, together with the sense of redemption that women seemed to experience after saying them out loud, prompted Ensler to expand what was once a private exercise into a global mission. The nonprofit organization she established, V-Day, has become a multimillion-dollar undertaking, now working in 140 countries to "end violence against women and girls" through multiple means, both artistic and concrete.[25] In 2011 Ensler was chosen by *Newsweek* and *The Daily Beast* as one of "150 Women Who Shake the World,"[26] as well as

24. Eve Ensler, *The Vagina Monologues*, tenth anniversary edition (New York: Villard Books, 2008), xliii.

25. For details go to V-Day's web site, www.vday.org/home.

26. http://blogs.thedailybeast.com/interactive/women-in-the-world/150-women-who-shake-the-world/?om+rid=MSvLrF&om_mid=_BNdNzoB8Zf4005.

earning a place on the list of *The Guardian*'s "Top 100 Women" for her activism.[27] Her recent accomplishments include the new construction of the City of Joy, a center for victims of genocidal rape in the Democratic Republic of Congo.[28] Many women who have encountered one of the thousands of performances of the monologues have, for the very first time, heard someone give voice to their own embodied experiences of menstruation, rape, childhood sexual abuse, sexual harassment, genital cutting, body hatred, or childbirth. As Gloria Steinem put it, "Women's sanity was saved . . . by bringing these hidden experiences into the open, naming them, and turning rage into positive action."[29] While not every audience member finds this redemptive, some are inspired to become activists themselves.

The response to Ensler's work has not all been positive, of course; indeed, many people have found it horrifying. It has been attacked from multiple sides—by feminists for, among other things, reducing women to a body part that is not even properly identified[30]; by artists for writing a piece of aesthetically worthless junk posing as theater; and by LGBTQ critics for being too heteronormative in its focus. Perhaps its most vehement critics, though, have been Christians. At a most basic level Christians of many stripes find the play's language and subject matter crude; more substantive critiques charge (not without reason) that the play deliberately undermines traditional biblical or Christian norms of gender and sexuality.[31] Such qualms have led a number of col-

27. Katharine Viner, "Top 100 Women: Eve Ensler," *The Guardian* (March 8, 2011): www.guardian.co.uk/books/2011/mar/08/eve-ensler-100-women.

28. V-Day web site, www.vday.org/node/2649 (originally from Jeffrey Gettleman, "Fighting Congo's Ills with Education and an Army of Women," *New York Times* [February 6, 2011], 6.)

29. From Steinem's introduction to *The Vagina Monologues*, tenth anniversary edition, (New York: Villard, 2008 [1998]), xxxiii.

30. Harriet Lerner, "'V' is for Vulva, Not Just Vagina," *Lawrence Journal-World and News* (May 4, 2003): www2.ljworld.com/news/2003/may/04/v_is_for.

31. For a more thorough survey of Christian critiques, see Kathryn D. Blanchard, "Who's Afraid of *The Vagina Monologues*?: Christian Responses and Responsibilities to Women on Campus and in the Global Community," in

lege administrators to ban, or attempt to ban, the play from being performed on religiously affiliated campuses; nevertheless, the number of performances of *The Vagina Monologues* around the world continues to climb steadily each year. Even a few seminaries and congregations have made it part of their "liturgical" calendars.

Where we believe this play dovetails nicely with the practice of women's biblical interpretation is in their shared concern with what Steinem calls the "journey of truth telling."[32] To a significant degree, biblical exegesis has always been about readers finding themselves in Scripture, preferably in ways that validate the particulars of their own existence and experience. Those who suffer have found stories of suffering that offer hope of redemption; those who are wealthy find justification for their wealth; those whose lives have been changed by the experience of the divine find precedence for these experiences among scriptural characters. *Lady Parts* is no different in this regard. Naomi Graetz writes, "For the Bible to be kept alive, it must be remolded on a regular basis. The midrashic process has to continue. In every generation there are those who feel the legitimate need to re-interpret the Bible and to demonstrate its relevance—a sort of renewing of the covenant. In this generation it is women who feel this need."[33] It should be said that not all of the monologues here are focused on or even mention vaginas. This is because responses to both *The Vagina Monologues* and the Bible are as varied as the women who encounter them; not all authors have chosen to present the vagina as the primary locus of embodiment.

This approach of applying what might be called "vagina lenses," while at the same time allowing readers' own womanly experiences as daughters, sisters, lovers, or mothers to inform their interpretations of the biblical texts, can bring to light surprising exegetical and social issues, both past and current. Take,

Journal of the Society of Christian Ethics 30/2 (2010) 99–122.

32. *The Vagina Monologues*, tenth anniversary edition, xxxiii.

33. Naomi Graetz, *S/He Created Them: Feminist Retellings of Biblical Stories* (Piscataway, NJ: Gorgias Press, 2003), 2.

for example, the case of Bathsheba: was she a seductress or a rape victim? The answers to such questions necessarily depend upon one's interpretive lenses, so women-in-the-Bible volumes are quite divided as a result. Some volumes exonerate Bathsheba completely, such as the 1849 volume that says she was "more sinned against than sinning" and that "we should probably feel more for her of compassion than of blame."[34] Others understand it as a case of adultery, a joint effort between David and Bathsheba. One monologue has Bathsheba saying, "That night is all a blur. Oh, if only I hadn't been bathing that evening!"; later she says her son with David died "for *our* sin."[35] Another even less sympathetic interpretation puts it this way: "There are two people involved in this conception: David and Bathsheba. Many people who read this story want the story to say that . . . Bathsheba had no choice in the matter . . . But note that Bathsheba responds to her pregnancy by [aligning herself with] David . . . Many people speculate that her name is not included in [Jesus'] genealogy because . . . murder and collusion and profit from evil are part of her story."[36] One monologue written in David's voice erases Bathsheba from the story altogether, neglecting even to mention her, instead stating pathetically in David's bewildered voice, "Sorrow and conflict seemed to plague me constantly . . . the heart-rending loss of my infant child, and then my son Absalom!"[37]

Visual art goes even further in its repudiation of Bathsheba: In his 1889 painting, *Bathsheba,* Jean Leon Gérôme presents her fully naked on an open rooftop; she is turned to the sun—and to David—and her chest is illumined; her voluptuous hip is hitched up in a traditionally provocative pose. She stands in the center

34. William B. Sprague (ed.), *Women of the Old and New Testaments* N(ew York: D. Appleton., 1849), 226.

35. Gartner, *Meet Bathsheba*, 61, 63. Emphasis added.

36. Megan McKenna, *Not Counting Women and Children: Neglected Stories from the Bible* (Maryknoll, NY: Orbis, 1994), 113. The Gospel of Matthew 1:6 refers to her as "Uriah's wife."

37. Kenneth W. Osbeck, *52 Bible Characters Dramatized: Easy-to-Use Monologues for All Occasions* (Grand Rapids, MI: Kregel, 1996), 89.

of a very subtle "v," a symbol of a fertile woman, created by the black shadowy woman on the left and the white garment on the right; black and white come together at her feet, suggesting that she has power. Furthermore, the angle of the kneeling woman and the pointed tower direct both Bathsheba's and the observer's gaze to David. She seems to be inviting his attention.[38] In sum, because of the vast differences of cultural circles and individual circumstances that shape different biblical interpretations, heterogeneous readings of Bathsheba have existed long before now.

Even if interpreters do not declare Bathsheba to be an *active* conspirator in David's sin, many hesitate to name her experience "rape," a contemporary phenomenon that is both radically different from, and deeply continuous with, the biblical context. To some readers it is obvious. As Trevor Dennis writes in *Sarah Laughed*, "Bathsheba's vulnerability emerges from the text before she gets there. The king can see her bathing. He is in a position to invade her privacy. Her nakedness is explored. Unknowingly, even before she is summoned to the king's presence, she is thus humiliated and put to shame."[39] Another book, *Flawed Families of the Bible*, says, "It is simply male fantasy to think that women are being seductive when they are in fact being exploited; . . . Even if there was no physical struggle, even if she gave in to him, it was rape."[40] Other readers, however, prefer not to use such a

38. For a more in-depth analysis of this image, see Lynn R. Huber, Dan W. Clanton Jr., and Jane S. Webster, "Biblical Subjects in Art," pages 197–228 in *Teaching the Bible Through Popular Culture and the Arts* (edited by Mark Roncase and Patrick Gray; Atlanta, GA: Society of Biblical Literature, 2007), 197–198.

39. Trevor Dennis, *Sarah Laughed: Women's Voices in the Old Testament* (Nashville, TN: Abingdon, 1994), 145.

40. Diana R. Garland and David E. Garland, "Bathsheba's Story: Surviving Abuse and Loss," *Family and Community Ministries: Empowering through Faith*, 21. 3 (2007) (chapter excerpt from *Flawed Families of the Bible: How God's Grace Works through Imperfect Relationships* [Grand Rapids, MI: Brazos, 2007]), 23, 25. For a fuller treatment of rape in the Bible, see Susanne Scholz, *Sacred Witness: Rape in the Hebrew Bible* (Minneapolis, MN: Fortress, 2010); see pp. 83–103 for her description of Bathsheba's rape as an issue of controlling wives and marital rape fantasies.

strong word and may instead try to soften it as an example of abuse of power or sexual harassment (more akin, say, to Bill Clinton and Monica Lewinsky). Interpretation here is made trickier by the fact "no legal or technical term for rape exists in Biblical Hebrew," and thus English translators have to use context to determine when "rape" might be the appropriate translation.[41] And even if there *were* a tidy linguistic term meaning "rape" in Hebrew, what if the biblical author did not choose to use this term, and instead used a more general term for "to lie with"? Some readers' operating assumption is that if the author of this story didn't consider it rape, then it was not rape; but is this necessarily true to Bathsheba's embodied experience? Such hesitancy to call this situation rape is not unique to male readers; in *Really Bad Girls of the Bible*, Liz Curtis Higgs says to those who would call it rape, "Oh dear, do we have to go there? . . . There's no question that David started this skin game, but there's also not a word in the text that suggests Bathsheba put up a fight."[42]

While there is no way to offer a satisfactory verdict on this particular question, the point for the moment is that even an amateur's exegesis, informed by *The Vagina Monologues* and arising from her own critical engagement with ambiguities and gaps in the biblical text, can create the occasion for enlightening discussion about the definition of rape—not just in the Bible, but also in our own day. Such discussions about violence against women, among secular people and people of faith alike, are more than merely academic exercises.[43] They also have deep and im-

41. Gravett, "Reading 'Rape,'" 279.

42. Liz Curtis Higgs, *Really Bad Girls of the Bible* (Colorado Springs, CO: Water Brook, 2000), 142. Later she notes that the text, "does not say 'The thing *Bathsheba* had done displeased the Lord.' Ah, that may be our biggest clue that she had little choice in all the sinful proceedings" (149).

43. Recently an American woman, who as a teenager was raped and impregnated by a fellow church member, finally spoke up about how she had been forced by her parents and pastor to stand up and apologize in front of the entire congregation for being raped, before being hidden somewhere across the country to bear her child in shame. See Trent Spiner, "Police: Girl raped,

mediate practical importance to those of us studying or working at institutions of higher education, where there currently exists a nationwide "plague" of unreported and/or unpunished sexual assaults against female students by their male colleagues (sometimes called "date rape"), largely because the parties involved disagree on the nature of what happened.[44] Such brutal realities in the so-called developed world, to say nothing of the ongoing tragedies women and girls experience in regions where warlords have overtaken the rule of law, act as painful reminders that women—or perhaps more precisely, humans with vaginas—do not yet experience full equality with most humans with penises.

As a strategy for teaching biblical studies, we the editors find that the approach of combining midrash with *The Vagina Monologues* works well because it combines two already existing and complementary pedagogical traditions, one old and well established, one young and controversial. Take Norma Gangel Rosen's explanation of midrash, which could almost as easily have been written about *The Vagina Monologues*: she writes, "Midrash is not a fairy tale of happily ever after, but a delving into deeper reality that allows the thorns to remain in place. Spirit and flesh are still torn. Not poultice, but *naming torn places* is what brings relief—or revives our resolution to live in the tension of no relief."[45] By the same token, Eve Ensler's reasoning for *The Vagina Monologues* could be easily applied to feminist midrash: she writes, "If we are going to end violence against women, the whole story has to change. We have to look at shame and humiliation and poverty and racism and what building an empire on the back of the world does to the people who are bent over. We

then relocated," *Concord Monitor* (May 25, 2010), www.concordmonitor.com/article/police-girl-raped-then-relocated?page=0%2C1.

44. The term "plague" was used in a series of National Public Radio reports about campus rape (*Morning Edition*, February 24, 2010); available through the Center for Public Integrity, "Sexual Assault on Campus," online: www.publicintegrity.org/investigations/campus_assault/.

45. Norma Gangel Rosen, *Biblical Women Unbound: Counter-Tales* (Philadelphia, PA: Jewish Publication Society, 1996), xii-xiii. Emphasis added.

have to say that what happens to women matters to everyone and it matters A LOT."[46] Both midrash and *The Vagina Monologues*, in other words, are about storytelling, especially where there are gaps or "torn places" in the stories. What both movements share is the conviction that women's stories, whether in the Bible or real life, are *human* stories that must be heard in order for the world to be made whole.

Naming Torn Places, with Fear and Trembling

What follows is a collection of monologues in the voices of biblical women written by modern women in conversation with both the Bible and *The Vagina Monologues*. Most of the authors are non-specialists and total newcomers to biblical exegesis; most are also new to creative writing. As a result, readers may find the text surprisingly rough, even vulgar in places. We believe, however, that the unpolished or "amateurish" character of the collection is appropriate to our attempt to engage Eve Ensler's work—itself criticized for not meeting the standards of high art set by experts. Even so, we recognize and appreciate the authentic depth of poetry and art written into these stories. We also affirm our pedagogical conviction that biblical exegesis is a potentially beneficial exercise for all people, not only for those with scholarly or professional credentials.[47] Most people, in our experience, are grateful for the opportunity and permission to read, and especially to question, the Bible they were handed. Some of the authors in this group were religious studies majors, some making sense of their Christian upbringing; others were agnostics or avowed atheists, wanting little or nothing to do with religion. Writers range in age from the twenties to the sixties; they are black, white, and Latina; and they

46. Ensler, *The Vagina Monologues*, xx-xxi.

47. For a recent justification of the usefulness of performance in teaching the Bible, see David Torbett, "'I Did Not Wash My Feet with That Woman': Using Dramatic Performance to Teach Biblical Studies," *Teaching Theology and Religion* 13/4 (2010) 307–319.

vary in sexual orientation and marital status. But all of the writers have empowered themselves by actively engaging with the book that has shaped Western civilization more than any other.

Many of the monologues in this volume are intensely personal; they have been shaped not only by canonical texts but also, and perhaps more importantly, by the experiences of the authors. All were willing and able to bring themselves and their experiences into dialogue with the texts in ways that were fruitful for them. While these monologues are fictional and should certainly not be taken as autobiographies, the authors have nevertheless chosen to write on particular characters with whom they identified or who spoke to them in some important way. They have used their own experiences with sexual abuse, oppression, conflicted friendships, economic discrimination, gender, menstruation, celibacy, infertility, motherhood, and menopause to inform their interpretation of the ancient stories about these and other topics. They have allowed their own (or their sisters', mothers', or friends') joys, sorrows, angers, fears, and triumphs to shape the words of the biblical women. They have wrestled with their identity as women, their relationships, and their understandings of human suffering. For many of the authors, the process has therefore been not only educational in terms of biblical knowledge, but also existential—bringing catharsis and healing. Needless to say, for some writers the process of "naming torn places" was extremely difficult and emotionally draining.

This process has also been profoundly theological. Authors had to wrestle with not only the biblical texts but also directly with the God—sometimes cruel, sometimes kind, sometimes utterly silent—who emerges from their pages. This means that some of the monologues may seem unfinished or biblically "incorrect" to well-informed readers of the Bible. Nevertheless, where the authors' own theological and existential issues are unresolved, so too are some of the painful situations in their monologues. As poet Alicia Ostriker puts it, the Bible is an "open book," which is "to say that anyone may read it, that anyone may enter its chapter and verse. It is there . . . for all to see"; people should therefore be encouraged to "read the Bible not as they have been officially taught, but for themselves, with their own eyes and minds."[48] This approach is dangerous, perhaps, but also necessary and, finally, inevitable.

The editors and authors are painfully aware that the nature of this volume may make us vulnerable to severe criticism from certain quarters; Eve Ensler took a lot of heat for her play, and we have dared to add the fan of religion to the flame of vaginas. For some of us, this has been a process undertaken with much fear and trepidation. The institutions where we work are not located in New York or San Francisco (where sexual liberty and theological skepticism are *de rigueur*), but primarily in the Midwest and the South, neither of which is known for radical theology, feminism, or iconoclasm. Moreover, some of the monologues contain thinly veiled autobiographical details that authors may or may not wish to share with friends, family, colleagues, or total strangers. Some of us are perfectly comfortable talking about vaginas in public; others are more comfortable using a wider focus on the whole body. But it must also be said that many of the monologues in *Lady Parts*, like *The Vagina Monologues* itself, can—indeed should!—be read with a sense of humor. Human beings have joked and laughed, however darkly, at a variety of human suffering, from the mildly sad (PMS) to the tragic (crucifixion) to the utterly horrific (the Holocaust). Sometimes gallows humor seems like the only way to address something painful, or at least it seems better than weeping. So if you detect a bit of sarcasm or irony in these monologues, you are probably not just imagining it. And if you feel like laughing now and then, go ahead. In the end, the editors believe in the project as a whole, and believe that there is plenty of room for the wide variety of approaches herein.

The following monologues are arranged in the order in which they are found in the Bible. The characters are listed by

48. Alicia Suskin Ostriker, *For the Love of God: The Bible as an Open Book* (New Brunswick, NJ: Rutgers, 2007), 1, 7.

their names or, in the many cases of nameless women, are identified by their textual relationships (e.g., "Jephthah's Daughter"). Out of respect for the various religious communities that use different parts of the Bible as scripture, we divide the collection into three sections. We use the term "Hebrew Bible" to refer to the Jewish Tanak or the Protestant Old Testament. We use the term "Deuterocanonical Books" to refer to the later Jewish religious writings included in the Greek Septuagint (but not the Hebrew Bible) that were called "Scripture" by early church leaders and are still included in the Catholic and Orthodox Old Testaments; Protestants, if they are even aware of this collection, call it the "Apocrypha." (Readers can find these books easily online.) We use the term "New Testament" to refer to the last portion of the Christian scriptures, originally written in Greek. A brief contextual introduction is included before each monologue. These are creative works that do not contain citations, but for those who wish to pursue more scholarly approaches to the interpretive questions that arise here, the bibliography at the end of the volume will help guide further reading. We certainly encourage readers to read these *Lady Parts* alongside their biblical counterparts; where there are radical departures in the stories, they are deliberate rather than accidental.

One biblical scholar has written that any question about what constitutes the "best translation" of the Bible comes down to the question, "Best for whom and for what?"[49] Such is surely also true with regard to interpretations and retellings of the Bible. This volume of vagina-inspired monologues defines the best retelling as one that does not look away from women's bodies or women's suffering, but seeks to promote the integrity and well-being of women and girls by, first and foremost, letting women speak their truths. Naming torn places does not mean that women must remain "victims"; to the contrary, naming is often a necessary step toward empowerment and, finally, justice. Our

49. Daniel J. Harrington, *Interpreting the Old Testament: A Practical Guide* (Collegeville, MN: Liturgical, 1981), 109.

strategy thus strives toward two overriding goals: the ancient desire to engage newcomers in the biblical texts in ways that are meaningful and even exciting to them, and the ongoing mission to end violence against women and girls.

PART I

Women in the Hebrew Bible

EVE

Dolly Van Fossan

One of the first humans in the Bible, Eve (Genesis 1–3), is probably most famous for two things: her creation out of Adam's rib, and her role in getting humankind kicked out of Eden. The shadowy character of Lilith—a woman said to have been made from the dust with Adam but who left him after refusing to submit to his superiority—does not appear in Genesis but can be found in extra-canonical Jewish (and other ancient Middle Eastern) folk sources. She helps, in part, to explain the discrepancies between the two creation stories in Genesis 1–2.

EVERYBODY ALWAYS WANTS TO know, "Why did you do it? Why did you allow yourself to be so easily deceived? What were you thinking as your teeth sank into that tempting, enigmatic fruit?" The questions madden me—not in themselves of course, but in the assumptions behind them: that I was stupid, or gullible, or passive; that I intentionally ruined things for everyone; that I caused the downfall of humankind; that I'm the reason half the population exists in subjugation.

I've seen the stories you've written about me—scriptures, "holy texts," as you call them. I've seen the pictures, the statues, the drawings that are supposed to bear my visage. I've heard your preachers speak of me; they do it with reluctance or disdain. Yet none of you—*none* of you—has ever heard *me*.

Oh sure, I get one or two lines in your stories. "The serpent beguiled me, oh Lord, and I ate!" And I'm cowering—because

33

I'm naked. Really? You don't think I was furious that all this time God was enjoying a personal peep show without my consent, or that the man tried to shove the blame onto me—as if he hadn't eaten from the tree too?

Alright, I'll tell you why I did it. I did it for *her*. I did it for *us*. We're in love. We've been in love ever since Adam over there couldn't befriend anything unless it was sliced out of his own gut. Talk about ego! And, of course, I'm brought to him, like some rib-eye steak on a silver platter, and he gets to name me, and I'm just expected to go along with the deal. As soon as I met him, I knew it wasn't going to work out. I mean, he'd complained to God about losing a rib but then was satisfied about the dusty banana dangling between his legs!

When I met her, she was just wandering the garden, as most creatures were prone to do. None of us—not even the animals— were entirely certain why we were there. God had declared that It created us and this was the Beginning. But given all Its issues— and trust me, It has issues—nobody really believed it. We just lived in this bland sprawl of garden: fruit trees, rivers, and each other. No fears, no pains, no heartbreaks—but no thrills, no joys, no bliss. I hate the art that my descendants created in imitation of me, but damn! What I would have given back then for even the most infuriating, lopsided, misinformed invective! Even if God created us, It didn't bother to consider the possibility that we would tire of being Its windup toys. Half the time, I think It gave us the capacity to reason just to see if we would dare defy It.

But she *loved* defying It. She took enormous pleasure in it. Almost from the moment she was created, it was one of her favorite pastimes. She, of course, had come before Adam. Yeah, I know what your stories say. You like to think Adam was the first "model." Unh, unh—*Lilith* was the first human being. And let me tell you, she was one helluva bitch.

God had created her as an experiment. It was satisfied until that point with Its animals aimlessly wandering around. Lilith, though, was God's answer to Its own loneliness. It created her not from the brilliance of Its own perfection, but from the madness of pure, undiluted solitude. The cacophony of questions in Its head: Where was Its creator? Why did It exist? Why the nothingness? The earth It created was somewhat placating, but God still wanted answers, and so It created Lilith from the dust and breathed life into her.

Lilith didn't have any answers for God. She didn't particularly seem to care about how or why the world was constructed, or that her own creator was caught up in some existential crisis. She was adventurous, totally intrepid. She wanted to live life to the fullest for as long as it lasted. So when God told her, "You may freely eat of every tree of the garden; but of the tree of knowledge of good and evil you shall not eat, for in the day that you eat of it, you shall die"—well, it was like God had drawn a map to her first destination.

Of course she ate the fruit! She had no idea what death was! Did God assume she would be terrified of an end to existence when Its own Being, Its own Existence, was so uncertain? When she ate, she became mortal and loved it. She knew Beauty. She knew Truth. She knew Love. She knew Feeling to the fullest.

God was pissed when It found out what Lilith had done. It tried to banish her from Eden permanently. But Lilith was already gone. She wasn't going to stick around with her new awareness. Who knows where she went? She just disappeared like that sometimes. It's part of her mysterious nature.

So God, finding Itself lonely again, tried a second model—Adam—to make up for the failure of Lilith. Of course, Adam turned out to be this passive, needy, whiny thing. God wanted obedience and It got it—but what's the value in obedience when it's mandated? Adam was a disappointment, another rough draft that still needed revisions. God wanted an equal, like Lilith, but one that It could control, like Adam.

And that's where I come in.

Adam was told that I was made for *him*. He still likes to imagine that. God, of course, was really just trying to deal with the guilt of abandoning the poor boy after creating him. Meanwhile, It's trying to get me to understand that It's my friend and It loves me unconditionally, but if I ever disobey It, I'll be cast forever out of paradise (or, as later folks would tell the story, damned to the fires of an eternal, demon-filled furnace). Yeah, no contradictions in that!

Lilith and I are more alike than Adam, though. Despite our disparate births, both of us have a streak of independence that God simultaneously loves and hates. She gave me the details on this creation workshop, the 101 on why I was created. She told me about the tree and the fruit. She was the one that convinced me to try it.

And oh hell, when I did—*everything came alive!* Her sweet, soft flesh, those supple, round, rolling curves, and a thick bush of curly dark hair (up there!). We made love under the watchful gaze of snake eyes, on the premium grounds of paradise. I knew then that whatever suffering I was in store for would be worth it—anything for a taste of Lilith's honey.

Adam tried the fruit on his own at some point. It was kind of inevitable, really. I didn't have to do anything to "seduce" him. Living with the prospect of never dying is a terror all its own. Adam couldn't understand the known, never mind the unknown. So why not give mortality a try?

Needless to say, God was PO'd. Seriously mad. And really immature too. It gets all childish about the whole thing and banishes us from the garden. Tells Adam he's gonna eat dust and I'm gonna have a hard time having babies. Like we didn't realize pain came with the deal when we ate from the tree. God wouldn't even *speak* to Lilith. It thought by giving her the cold shoulder It was making a statement or something. She didn't care. She stayed by my side, nibbling my earlobe, making me giggle while God went off on Its tirade.

So, we left.

We went wandering to find ourselves a new home. We didn't need God. God could figure Itself out, while we did the same for ourselves. I'll admit, I ended up getting a bit bi-curious with Adam. Lilith wasn't too wild about it until he suggested a threesome. We had some of the issues you might expect with polyamory, but once the kids came around it wasn't so bad. A couple of fig leaves helped.

Where are we now? Can't really say. Divine confidentiality agreements, you know? But I can tell you that I've never regretted my choice. Not once. Lilith and I love each other with a relentless passion that has only flourished since we left the garden. Each tender kiss on her exquisite lips reminds me of that, along with each gentle caress, each warm embrace, each soothing smile. She woos me with the charm of a thousand suitors. She reads my thoughts, my fears, my dreams. She shares them with me fully; she holds me in the night. I love her; she loves me; we love each other.

And I'm here to tell you that if you think *I* was the one that made you all have your wars and rapes and hate crimes and whatever other oppressive shit you have going on now, think again. Life begins and ends with Love; it's only God that stands in the way of your happiness and your harmony.

Hagar and Sarah

Kathryn D. Blanchard

Hagar and Sarah are most famous for being the mothers of Abraham's two sons, Ishmael and Isaac, respectively. Sarah is somewhat notorious for being infertile, encouraging her husband to produce an heir with her slave, Hagar, and then banishing Hagar and Ishmael out of jealousy (Genesis 16); later she bears her own son, Isaac, whom Abraham nearly sacrifices (Genesis 21–22). Hagar, meanwhile, is the only person in the Bible to give God a name (Genesis 16), and she, like Abraham, is promised a great multitude of descendants.

Sarah

If you ask me about my vagina, you'd better be prepared to hear a sad story. First of all, I had to marry my half-brother. He had never been particularly bad or particularly good to me; he mostly either teased me or ignored me, the way big brothers do. He started to look at me a little differently, though, first when I got breasts—really nice ones, mind you—and then later when I started bleeding and it was time for me to be married off. For a while after we married he wanted to have sex constantly. Sometimes he hurt me a lot, but I don't think it was on purpose. He just didn't have a clue how to please a woman—couldn't find a clitoris to save his life. He never asked me what I liked, so in general I didn't like it much at all. Every now and then, though, he would come to me with these crazy stories about how he'd had a visit from his god; he'd be wild-eyed with all these promises his god had made to him about us having lots of offspring and land. Sometimes the sex was even good then; something about his crazy look actually turned me on—got me wet enough that I could enjoy myself. But whenever my next period arrived he would get that scary look and I knew what was coming.

Hagar

If you ask me about my vagina, you'd better be prepared to hear a sad story. Things started out kind of all right back in Egypt. I had a loving mother, a loving grandmother. But before I became a woman I was sold to this immigrant. They just took me away one day; I didn't even get to say my goodbyes. I wanted to cry but I didn't have any tears. Instead I just felt empty, like a ghost. When I first met her, she looked as sad as I felt. Being her hand-maid actually turned out to be okay, at least for a while. She didn't have any kids, so she seemed kind of glad to have me around; she kind of became like a mother to me. When I had my first period, she was there to tell me what to do, to teach me how cold water gets the blood out of cloth better than hot. I don't think she really had any other friends, and she hated her husband because of what he did to her back in Egypt. Maybe we wouldn't have *chosen* each other as friends, but we were kind of thrown together so we made the best of it.

Sarah

There were some especially dark times for my vagina, namely when my husband told people I was his sister, while conveniently neglecting to mention that we were married. People have always told me I am quite beautiful. 'Lotta good that ever did me. Once

Lady Parts

I was taken into Pharaoh's household. That's the nice version of the story. The truth is that my husband pimped me out, *he said* because he feared for his life, but really it was to make himself rich. He was very handsomely paid, and sent off with a scolding and a wink. The only good that came out of Egypt for me was her—I didn't realize how badly I'd needed a friend.

Hagar

There were some especially dark times for my vagina, namely when she gave me to her husband to have his baby. For years she'd been telling me how much she hated him. How greedy he was in bed. How uncomfortable sex was. The most terrifying part for me was that he was crazy—he would get these visions where he would talk to his god, and then he'd fly around yelling about how he'd been promised lots of children. She said sometimes he hit her when she bled, because she was failing to fulfill his god's promise. I guess she threw me to the lion to get herself some relief. I was scared and wanted to refuse but, as a slave, what choice did I have? The first time he summoned me to his bed was awful. He had trouble getting inside me because I was a virgin, so he used his fingers until I broke. I wanted to cry but I didn't have any tears. When I left, I noticed the bed had these bloody marks on it. Funny—I remember there wasn't nearly as much blood as I thought there would be; not enough to reveal how much my poor vagina had just suffered.

Sarah

If you want to know the truth, I'm not sure I ever really wanted to be a mother. I mean, I always figured I would be—just because that's what people do—but I couldn't tell you for sure whether I actually *desired* a child in those early years. It was more of an expectation. Not to have children was unthinkable; it meant the end of my family line, my religion, my culture. But it was mostly something *he* wanted—not me. So then I had this idea to let him have a baby with her. She'd been with me about ten years, since the first time he rented out my vagina. She and I were quite close; maybe not soul mates, but close the way women get when they're thrown together all day every day. We were kind of like sisters. We even bled around the same time each month. I thought if he and I had a baby through her he would leave me alone. So I gave her to him as a wife.

Hagar

If you want to know the truth, I'm not sure I ever really wanted to be a mother. Or maybe it's more accurate to say that I never had time to think about it. I was so young. I think the gods must have had mercy on me, because I got pregnant the very first month; he had to come to me eight times and that was it. She knew I was pregnant even before I did—she came to ask me if I was bleeding yet, and I wasn't. Then she said to me one day, "Look how big your breasts are." All I could think about was taking a nap. She seemed quieter than usual, but she was so interested in me being pregnant that I started to think maybe it was pretty cool after all. Plus, when he found out, he was so excited that he took *her* gold amulet and gave it to *me* to ward off the evil eye. Still, it all didn't seem real until I felt the baby kicking. That was the moment for me when I realized I was a living miracle—that my body was magically making another, separate body. I ran to her to tell her the first time he kicked, and that was when she told me that I should stop bragging.

Sarah

I didn't expect how I would feel when she got pregnant. First of all, her breasts got huge, and she had this sort of glow about her, always rubbing her fucking belly, gloating even while complaining about the morning sickness, saying she couldn't help me with any housework because she was too tired, yadda yadda. I'm ashamed to say it, but that was the first time I ever *really* wanted to be pregnant. I wanted to feel beautiful and fertile and voluptuous; instead I felt like a dried up old bag, a tree with no fruit. My mistake, of course, was to share these feelings out loud. I should have kept it to myself I suppose, but I've always been someone who has to get stuff off my chest. When I admitted to her how I was feeling, I could tell she started to pity me. She made it so obvious, always looking at me with her eyebrows raised in false concern—*oh, poor thing*. Like I was some pathetic object of contempt. It hurt a lot because of course I already pitied myself. I walked around in a fog, feeling really raw but trying to keep my head held high. I guess I didn't succeed though. I've never been all that good at hiding it when I'm upset.

Hagar

I didn't expect how she would feel when I got pregnant, not that I had any choice in the matter. After the baby started kicking and my belly got big enough for all to see, she really changed. You could see the jealousy and anger all over her face whenever she looked at me. Her nostrils flared; her jaw clenched. I honestly started to feel sorry for her; she'd been someone I'd always looked up to, and now she was behaving like a child. It was pathetic. Finally, one day when she'd been especially ridiculous, I burst out and told her to grow up—that it was *her* fault I was pregnant in the first place, that it wasn't *my* fault that I was fertile or that she was frigid. I guess I went a bit too far, because she actually jumped on me—pulling my hair, scratching my face, calling me names. Of course we were so loud that everyone came running.

Sarah

I felt ganged up on, so I lost it. My bastard of a husband scolded me like a child, saying that I should grow up and that it was my own fault anyway for being so cold to him in bed. I so desperately wanted to hurt both of them. I wanted to punch the smug pregnant smile off her smug pregnant mouth, kick his proud, baby-making balls so hard he'd never even think of putting himself in a woman again. Instead I called down the curse of his promise-making god on his head. I guess that scared him a little. He didn't actually apologize, of course, but he backed down and told me I could do whatever I wanted with "my slave" and then walked off in a huff.

Hagar

I felt ganged up on, so I ran. She was way out of line, and he barely even tried to stand up for me. But I did feel somewhat guilty about the things I'd said to her. I tried to put myself in her place, feeling like a failure, wanting a baby so desperately. I was surprised at how much I was looking forward to having a child of my own, a person in the world who would love *me* even when no one else did. I already knew this baby was going to be the love of my life. She didn't have that. Still, I was well on my way back to Egypt, and don't think I would have gone back to her if El-Roi hadn't seen me in the desert, if I hadn't seen him. He told me to go back to her, flawed as she was. And then he said almost the same thing that crazy man was always saying—that if I did what he said I would have so many offspring no one could ever count them. He said I was having a son and that his name was Ishmael—"god hears." I can hardly believe it now, but I did go back. Somehow, knowing that god saw me—had been watching me, even in my darkest hours—it made all my pain seem important. Productive even. Like my vagina and I were part of something bigger.

Sarah

Ishmael's birth was bittersweet. I'd felt pretty guilty after she ran away. She'd been a good friend up until then—my only friend, really—and I was relieved to see her when she came back. We cried and hugged each other and said we were sorry, but things had changed between us. She seemed older now somehow; like she was the big sister and I was the younger; like she had some secret knowledge that I'd never have. I still felt jealous, I can't deny it, but I remembered that she was having this child for me and tried to think of it as my own. So I labored with her, held her between my knees when she gave birth to Ishmael, and for a while I almost felt like he was my son too. But even then, I still wanted a baby of my own. Ishmael liked me, but—even if I didn't have the vivid memory of watching him emerge all squashed and gooey from between her legs—it was clear who his real mother was.

Hagar

Ishmael's birth was terrifying. I had never known what pain was until then. I remembered all the stories I'd heard about babies dying before they were born, or people bleeding to death before they even got their babies out. Still, the women around me made me feel like I could do it. They kept telling me that my body was doing everything just right—that my pain was normal, the blood was normal, the vomiting was normal, the shit coming out of me was normal. She was actually wonderful during my labor. She held me and rubbed my back hard during the contractions. She put cool rags on my forehead and whispered kind things to me about how miraculous I was. I kept reminding myself of El-Roi's promise that I would have countless children. It's kind of a blur now, but somehow Ishmael was born. He was perfect, every last bit of him. For a while after Ishmael came, things were pretty good between her and me. She was a big help with him, especially when he was really little. The older he got, though, the more distant she got, and eventually she went back to clenching her jaw, furrowing her brow, crying into her pillow at night.

Sarah

His god kept making promises about me having a baby, so he came to me every month, for years and years, right on schedule. Then every month when I got the cramp in my side, I felt like his god was mocking me. I was constantly counting days—first the days after my period, then the days till I bled again. The sex was terrible, as you can imagine; it was totally perfunctory, with this sad sense of resignation about it. One time I actually conceived; I went three months without bleeding and we were all ecstatic. But then I miscarried. The pain was so bad, and then I felt this weird urge to push, like I'd always imagined it would be to deliver a baby—god mocking me again. Finally a giant blood clot kind of slipped out of me; that's what I got for my labor—a dead blob of a baby that went out with the trash. She held me between her knees while I cried till there were no tears left in me. Years later, after I'd totally given up on having a child, the bleeding stopped again. I was getting older so I figured I was going through the change. My periods, which used to run rich and red and right on schedule, were now brown and clumpy and sporadic. I remember it because it was not long after these weird men came to visit us. They said I was going to conceive, which at the time made me laugh with bitterness because I'd heard it so many times before. My husband heard me laugh and got that crazy look that scares me so much. But I guess he didn't believe it either, because not long after that he had this great idea to rent out my vagina again, this time to the king of Gerar, who then play-acted that he was shocked to find out that I was married, and claimed loudly that he hadn't touched me. Again my husband got a public slap on the wrist, just for appearances; again he was handsomely paid. The only thing that made it all bearable was—well, you can guess.

Lady Parts

It's almost funny, really: his promised son was probably not even his. First my breasts got sore; then the nausea came; my labia were extra sensitive; and eventually my belly began to swell. My husband didn't know about it until well after I'd started to feel my baby kicking. One day he asked, out of the blue, why was I laughing so much lately? I told him it was a private joke he wouldn't understand. When my son finally arrived he was so tiny and vulnerable, so warm and sweet smelling. As if I needed one more reason to hate my husband, he took away my tiny, perfect baby and cut his tiny, perfect penis. He said his god had told him to do it.

Hagar

His god kept making promises about her having a baby. I was genuinely happy for her when she started showing. It felt nice to be able to pay her back some of the kindnesses she'd done to me when I had Ishmael—doing extra chores when she was so tired and swollen, helping her through her long labor, helping take care of the baby so she could get some rest now and then. It was probably the best time in our relationship since the really early years. But it didn't last long. Ishmael was growing up, acting like boys do, and she was always getting onto him and criticizing my parenting—said I wasn't strict enough with him, I coddled him, let him run wild. She was always so damn concerned about *her* son, her precious little prince. She spoiled him rotten, always giving into his cries and whines, always taking less for herself so he could have more, and yet she still had the nerve to criticize *me*! As if *my* son, the child of *my* womb, wasn't every bit as worthy as hers! I would never have admitted this at the time, but when he was being naughty, half the time I didn't discipline him just out of spite.

Sarah

I couldn't believe how much I loved my child. It was almost terrifying. We called him Isaac—"laughter"—my little private joke, the love of my life. I loved the feeling of him pulling my milk out of my breasts, even when it hurt—it made me feel like a real goddess, to be able to feed him from my own body, to be able to comfort him when he cried, to put him to sleep. I couldn't keep my hands off him; I always wanted to touch his soft hair, his impossibly smooth skin, the sweet nape of his neck. Sometimes I was so overwhelmed with desire that I wanted to put him in my mouth and consume him. As he got older, he started to get his own personality; he had a funny little sense of humor, always kept me laughing. But around the time that Isaac was born, Ishmael started acting out. He was getting to be a teenager, a wild ass of a young man. This had been a point of tension between her and me, because she didn't control her son the way she should have, despite my talking to her repeatedly about him playing too roughly with the baby. In her eyes, Ishmael could do no wrong, but I grew more and more afraid of him. The final straw was at Isaac's weaning celebration near his third birthday. It might have been partly my fault—I was already grieving about losing his babyness; I could actually feel the sadness in my nipples. So I was kind of on edge. But I saw Ishmael—who Isaac utterly worshipped, by the way—bullying Isaac and laughing when he cried out. She was standing right there and, as usual, did nothing, and I snapped. I hadn't lost it like that since she was pregnant. I told my husband that she and her son had to go. Honestly, though, I didn't expect him to give in the way he did. If I had known he was going to give in, I probably never would have said it. But I forgot how crazy he was until it was too late.

Lady Parts

Hagar

I couldn't believe how much I loved my child. It was almost ter-rifying. So when we got exiled into the desert it was the absolute worst moment of my entire life, for so many reasons. Ishmael was devastated to be cast out by his father, right at that age when a boy especially needs a man around. He wailed like I hadn't heard him wail since he was a child, and he pushed me away when I tried to comfort him. I could feel his sadness in my own body, like knives. On top of this emotional turmoil, the wilderness seemed to have turned hostile; our measly supplies had quickly run out before we had found a safe place to settle. In desperation, I left my grieving, dying son in what little shade I could find and then went looking for water, all the while crying out bitterly to El-Roi not to let my son die. Then suddenly, we were saved.

Sarah

There was no happily ever after for me and my vagina. I never had another friend like her. I learned to live with the physical sensation of loneliness, relieved only now and then for brief mo-ments when I got the ever-less-frequent hug from my ever-more-independent son. Then I lost even that. You probably know the rest of the story—his father did the unthinkable. Or he almost did, anyway, which is unthinkable in itself. One morning I woke up and Isaac and his father were gone, and no one would tell me where. After a day I started to freak out, and one of the servants I guess took pity on me and finally told me my husband had gone crazy and . . . I got this ringing in my ears, a cross between a battle cry and a screaming infant. I grabbed a ram and I started run-ning, planning to beg him for mercy. But when I got there and saw him with his knife held over my son's throat, I froze. I could see the end of the world. And then this scream came out of me from someplace way down deep—my husband's name. It didn't sound like my voice, didn't even sound human. After the horror,

I honestly couldn't think of one word to say to him that wouldn't somehow make him feel justified in his twisted little mind for what he'd done. So I said nothing to him ever again. I took my son and left for Hebron, while my husband stayed in Beersheba. But things were never the same between Isaac and me. Maybe he thought I had been part of his father's plan, or maybe he just realized how powerless I was to protect him. Even though he was physically there, I'd lost the intimate connection we'd once had. The old Isaac was gone, his laughter sacrificed on the altar of his father's self-importance. Grief joined loneliness as my only companions; they sat together like hungry ghosts on my chest. Sometimes I think a vagina is a curse—we watch life fight its way out of it, only to see that life move toward certain destruction.

Hagar

There was, unbelievably, a happily ever after for me and my vagina. You probably know the rest of the story—Ishmael and I stayed on the edge of the wilderness, near a life-giving well; he grew up into a fine man, an excellent hunter. When it came time, I did what good mothers do and found him a wife from my own people. They took good care of me, and I had more grandchildren and great-grandchildren than I can count. The only ending that wasn't happy was my breakup with her; the loss of that friendship was a wound that never really went away. I had known her so well, loved her for so long, and though our relationship had certainly been difficult at times, it was also powerful and warm and intimate, something I had depended on. When you're that close with someone for so long, you don't get over it quickly. But all in all, I'd have to say that things turned out pretty well. El-Roi saw me and my vagina, and blessed us for the ages.

BILHAH

Cate Pugliese

Bilhah (meaning "faltering" or "bashful" in Hebrew) first appears in Genesis 29:29, when Laban "gave his maid Bilhah to his daughter Rachel to be her maid." When Rachel struggles with infertility, she gives her servant Bilhah to Jacob as a wife in order to gain sons for herself. Bilhah bears two of Jacob's twelve sons, Dan and Naphtali. In chapter 35, after the death of Rachel, Jacob's son Reuben "lies with Bilhah" and his father hears of it. Bilhah herself never speaks in the Bible. According to legend, she is buried in the Tomb of the Matriarchs in Tiberias.

LABAN, THE SHEPHERD OF many, has come. She is told his name means white. She thinks of white as a place where there are no blemishes, where there is peace, and where she can go where there is no sin. But when he is here, white takes on darker hues.

It is now her turn to serve. He comes to her as he had Zilpah just seven short years before. This is a man whose name belies his purpose. Breathing. Wanting. Needing in a way that assumes possession. Even if asked, it wouldn't have been a permission granted—if he'd asked.

He has come again and I must leave. Although my body can't, my mind must.

I move toward the waves as they make their sounds again. Coming in and going out in a rhythm that is both calming and disquieting. I find myself walking on soft sand. I blink back the glare from the warm sun as its rays fall upon the parts of me. My legs look far away in the sun's spotlight. They feel even farther from my body.

With a name like Bilhah, she doubts everything about herself. She wavers constantly between shyness and insecurity, her only defenses in the face of others' greater strength.

In these moments of imagination, I continue my search. Each trip on this beach gives me something to look for, maybe even to look forward to. I watch my feet move through the foam toward the sand, watching to avoid stepping on unfound treasure, especially a sand dollar. One day I hope to find one unbroken. "Keep searching," I whisper to myself each time I take this walk.

I close my eyes imagining the rough exterior of the whole sand dollar, the one that is ready to be claimed by me. I haven't found it yet, but it will be mine. Searching means I am still on my beach and away from his needs. Untouched.

Untouched by the ebb and flow of the tide. Untouched by others who have come before. Untouched by the obstacles I know this shell must have encountered along its way as it arrives on my envisioned beach. It is pure, safe, and whole. Untouched.

Unlike who I am now.

She feels something push into her from outside. Pain shatters her body from within.

The sand dollar search.

Years ago, my sister Zilpah and I would search these same shores as young children, repeating to each other our mother's own words:

"Now break the center open, and here you will release,

The five white doves awaiting to spread Good Will and Peace."[50]

50. "The Legend of the Sand Dollar" is an anonymous poem popular among some Christians.

Is that what I will find? Good will? Peace?

I long to feel the velvety disc up against my cheek, sensing its façade of purity. Were good will and peace inside?

Finding something whole only to break it apart seems cruel.

My eyes scan the horizon of the beach, watching ahead to each careful step. Averting my eyes means missing my untouched treasure.

There it lies. I see my prize and I reach toward it . . .

She feels warmth and wetness, the sun's rays now gone.

My hand reaches toward the whole sand dollar. But as the waves crash, the sand slowly moves away and takes with it the dollar. I watch as it is raked across the rocks and broken. The waves are now silent. The ocean goes. Good will and peace leave. Wholeness departs.

The room comes back into focus. The walls are there now as is the carpet of straw for a bed beneath her. She looks down at her legs. Her body lies in front of her, yet apart from her.

She begins to take in the smells that are too familiar—musty, sweaty, darkly full of worry, if worry were a smell. The lingering stench of Laban—a man whose name now stains her soul with hues much darker than white—is on her. Perhaps he justifies this to himself, tells himself that he is readying her for her duty in his son-in-law's household.

She feels herself breathing in a way that tells her to stay still. She feels soreness in a place that should feel little, or nothing, at this time in her young life. Salty wetness seeps out of her and takes with it her ability to feel whole again.

Breathe. Remember to breathe. Try to get it back. But it is gone.

I pull up my garments and the wholeness of my strength. I hear now my family's mantra, God's promise to Abraham: "I will

surely bless you and make your descendants as numerous as the stars in the sky and as the sand on the seashore."
   At what cost will this promise unfold, I wonder?

JAEL

Emily Havelka

A tent-dwelling ally of Israel, Jael's claim to fame was the murder of Sisera, a Canaanite warrior (Judges 4). Having first offered him shelter and hospitality, she drove a tent peg into his temple while he slept, thereby robbing the Canaanites of their top military commander and delivering them into the hands of Israel's armies.

OH GREAT—MORE VISITORS HAVE come to congratulate me. "Good job, Jael! You've killed Sisera and saved Israel!" (Yeah, at least for the next ten minutes.)

Whoo-hoo.

"You must have been filled with the vengeful spirit of the LORD!" they say. "Our god is so great that even a lowly woman like you can strike down a mighty warrior with his strength!"

Is it really so hard to believe I just offed the guy, without needing some infusion of divine strength, or some big revelation?! There weren't any voices in my head saying anything to me about "avenging his people."

'Cause I would've remembered that.

This wasn't about Israel at all. It was about self-preservation, pure and simple. Why is it so difficult to believe that I was tired of living in fear? Why couldn't the fact that I acted on my own be divine in itself, without any special help from Yahweh?!

54

Just like all the others, he believed he was so entitled to everything . . . and everyone.

So he barges into my home, barking, "Water! Give me water!"

I was terrified!

So I gave him some milk to drink and he laid himself down to rest. Just lay there like this was his home, his tent! Like it was all his already! Of course I imagined what would come next.

You've heard the stories! What they do to the women!

Swooping in, killing everything . . . taking everything . . . "a womb, two wombs for every man."

And this man, a general . . . how many has he . . .

I'm not a womb.

I remember all those stories the women used to tell us— about their wars, about what happens to your life and everything in it, about what happens to you just for being a woman . . .

I'm not a womb.

It can't happen to me. He can't do that to me . . .

I'm not a womb.

I couldn't do it; I wouldn't let him!!!

I AM NOT A WOMB!!!!

I didn't do it for them, or their war; for Israel, or for Yahweh's supposed vengeance. I did it for me because no one else would. I saved myself because no one else would have even turned their head to look at my suffering . . .

Yet they seemed so surprised. When they saw my violence . . . They all looked at me like they were so surprised!

How many times had they walked in on one of my sisters, bleeding? Or dead and splayed out, legs all blackened, torn apart . . . nameless victims, easy to forget, nameless woman ruined at their feet . . . No surprise. No damned surprise.

But when they walked in on *him* lying there bleeding . . . big name, big famous name . . . Sisera, mighty general, penetrated and despoiled at MY feet . . . Surprise! Surprise! So damned surprised.

I guess they thought it was scary. To see someone important, someone with a name, lying there; to see someone so special, vanquished in hate by a mere woman, a nobody.

They recognized my violence, they understood it; it's all they have ever understood . . . and now they'll remember me. They'll record my name in their books.

"Yahweh! Yahweh! It's Yahweh's vengeance! It was foretold!"

But they're just trying to distract themselves . . . because they don't get to forget this time.

Because this time the one in the dirt is one of their kind. It's more convenient for them to believe it was some god acting through me. But they know the truth; they know what I did, and they know that *I* did it.

Jephthah's Daughter

Meredith Brown

Jephthah (Judges 11), at first an outlaw and outcast from Israel, later became their commander when they needed strong military leadership. In hopes of becoming Israel's top leader, he vowed to God that if God would help him defeat the Ammonites, he would sacrifice whoever came out of his house first to greet him upon his victorious return. The first one out of the house was his daughter, who remains unnamed in the text but who, according to the Bible, insists on helping him keep his vow.

I speak to you with cracked lips
unused, untouched and crusted over,
caked with the silence of centuries

They open now, slow as soil erosion
timid in their virginity
and speak words bitter and sharp like ginger roots;
these words will cut you as Jephthah cut me
they simmer like oil
evaporate like smoke.

I speak to you from a place in the afterlife
set aside for women
killed by their fathers
it is a cacophony of cramped quiet, here—

Lady Parts

we crawl over each other like
hatched larvae over rotten wood
sucked into ourselves, suckling, sympathetic
we all have our own calloused stories, and today
I will speak for you my own.

I am no patriarchal puppy.
I was raised by women
multiple mysterious mothers
who flitted into my life like gnats . . .
(and eventually were squashed by my father's fist)
they each tried to teach me the same thing:
listen, little girl, blend in with the men.
but on the inside grow like a weed in strength
plant your roots with silty women

I thrust my feet into their words
and it kept me from drip-draining out
of this world entirely

I can still leave water stains on a female heart.

This is how I was killed.
Jephthah was a fighter
who killed hundreds of people
in the name of a god
I did not know

Before his most important battle he made a vow.
I did not know what he promised.

I greeted him in dance
to celebrate his "victory" when he returned—
inside, I thought thousands of corpses might have also wanted
to dance with their daughters, someday

He approached slowly over a hill
He came closer, saying nothing
I stopped dancing, asked him
what's wrong?
He took me roughly by the arm
pincer fingers and
marched me to the valley
my childhood punishment place,
the place he'd take me if I was caught watching our sheep copulate
rough and loud
a look of awe creeping over my face as the bodies heaved

I asked him what I had done to displease him
and he snarled
stacked wood
bound my arms with thick tough rope
bound my feet
I was screaming and struggling but
no one heard me.

We were too far away.
He was too strong.

He lay me down on top of the wood
and as he set it on fire
he grabbed the blade tucked into his tunic and
cut me
cut into me
from neck to pelvis
I grew hot, my skin dripped
off the bone.

And then suddenly I was floating above myself and watched
as all of my friends danced angrily in the hills
stomping their feet and weeping

Lady Parts

for months, till they bled out,
women crushed with the knowing
that all we have ever been able to do is dance
and we do not even get to choose the beat.

LEVITE'S CONCUBINE

Jessica Paige

*Amidst the chaos in which Israel found itself, a concubine ran away
from her harsh Levite master and returned to her father's home in
Judah. (Judges 19) The Levite went to retrieve her, stayed on as a
guest of her father for a few days, and then set off toward his home
in Ephraim, taking the concubine with him. The situation deteriorates
when they have to spend the night among strangers in Benjaminite
territory.*

I wanted more. I needed more.
I needed an escape.

So I ran. I ran far from him.
I couldn't live with him anymore.
Under his roof, with his rules.
I needed an escape.

So I ran home to my father's house. For a while, I had my escape.
I was happy again. But then he came to me.
He wanted to "speak kindly to me."
He wanted me back in his house.
But he never spoke a word.

Lady Parts

For five days. Five days.
He and my father drank and they ate and they laughed.
But to me, not a single word.
I sat there for five days,
Waiting for him to take me back to that place
I didn't want to go. But I didn't have a choice.

So we left.
He, his servants, his donkeys, then me.
And we walked for hours. But not long enough.
The sun was setting and it was too dangerous.
So we stopped in Gibeah. And waited.
For someone, anyone, to take us in.

This old man took us in.
He trusted him; he was from his town.
The old man was supposed to take care of *us*.
But he only took care of *him*.

Then the mob came to the door.
They pounded, shouted, demanded.
They wanted him. And *only* him.
They wanted to rape him and hurt him.
They wanted *him*.

But that old man.
That damned. old. man.
He couldn't stand for such a thing to happen. Not to *him*.
So the old man offered them his daughter. And me.
He told them to take us.
He told them to do what they pleased.
He told them to do what they pleased, just not to his honored guest.
He told them to take us.

But they didn't want her. Or me.
They wanted him.
They demanded him.
They wanted HIM.
But he wouldn't allow it.
He wasn't going to be humiliated.

Then *he* grabbed my arm.
Dragged me through the house.
Her. Her. Take her.
I screamed and fought and tried and tried and tried.
He opened the door. Just enough so I could fit through.
He pushed me out the door.
HE pushed me out the door.

They took me somewhere.
Where, I do not know.
But they took their turns.
They each took turns.
Shoving things inside me.
Bottles and sticks and themselves.
They kept shoving things inside me.

I do not know how long they had me.
Or how many times they hit me.
Or how many men there were.
I cried and screamed and fought.

I never thought I would see the day again.
The sun broke, erased them.
And I ran far from there.
I ran back to him. Anywhere was better than there.
His house, the old man's house, the desert.
Anywhere but there.

Lady Parts

My body was moving, stumbling.
I couldn't feel my body, but it was moving.
I saw the door and stopped.
My body stopped moving.
My brain stopped moving.
I stopped. And my body gave way.

He almost tripped over me.
He left the house. He didn't know I was there.
He didn't know where I was.
And he didn't seem to care.
He almost tripped over me.
He yelled at me.
We were leaving he said.
Get up, he said. We're going.

I couldn't feel my legs or my lungs or my tongue.
Was I still alive?
I lay there. Waiting for him.
He picked up my body.
Weak, horrified, helpless.

He took my body to his house.
He laid me on his table.
I couldn't speak. Or move. Or see.
I lay there. Waiting for him.
He took his knife. He looked at my face.
And he cut me into pieces
Limb from limb from limb.
He tore me apart into twelve pieces,
One for each of Jacob's sons.
And I lay there. Waiting for him.

I wanted more. I needed more.
I needed an escape.

PENINNAH

Crystal Davis

*In the final chaotic years of the Judges, a wise and God-fearing proph-
et named Samuel would rule with justice; but when the people cried
out for a king, he obliged, and anointed first Saul and then David.
Where did Samuel come from? The story of his birth to Elkanah and
Hannah is told in 1 Samuel 1–2, and the story of Peninnah is found in
the cracks.*

I KNOW THE DREADFUL things you have heard about me. I know.
I also know that it is far from the truth! I am not the mean, nagging woman I have been made out to be. Of course, I have my
days, but who doesn't? The point is, I love my husband, and I
would do anything in the world for him. Wait! I *do* everything
for him! That is not the issue; it is my duty as his wife. The issue
is Hannah, the "other" wife. "Princess Hannah"—no, "Madame
Hannah." That woman sucks the life right out of me. Elkanah, my
husband, is married to the both of us: Hannah and me. Elkanah
and I have ten children together. Ten beautiful children. Elkanah
and Hannah have none. Hannah was unable to have children.

The fact that Elkanah and I have children together always
worked on Hannah's nerves. She was so cruel and nasty toward
me. I couldn't help that she couldn't have children; it wasn't my
fault. So why was she so hateful? She envied me, I know it. She
was constantly talking trash, bad-mouthing me. So, when I had

enough, I would lash out with what hurt her most: she could not have children, and I could; she was a worthless wife, with nothing to offer Elkanah. I know, harsh, but what was I to do? Let her get away with running all over me? She asked for it, and I was not going to back down. My words would hit her soul harder every time. She would sit around and sulk for days on end, while I had to take care of Elkanah, ten kids, and the cooking and cleaning, all on my own. She did nothing! Never lifted a finger. If I were not such a lady, I would have hit her square in the face. Maybe that would knock some sense into her, but it's doubtful.

Lord, listen to me carry on! The question is this: Why does my husband love her so dearly when all she cares about is herself? Yeah, she's beautiful; the type that makes you stop and stare. But looks aren't everything, I'm here to tell you! I was quite the catch back in my day, but after ten kids, and practically being a slave, you see what I am—the whole package! But he only loves her; I'm the "black shadow" when she is around. He should love me! ME! The one who loves him, the one who takes care of him, the mother of his children! So, why her? She has nothing to offer. He gives her everything! Even double portions of food at the sacrifice. I'm the one who has ten mouths to feed, plus my own. It makes me angry just talking about it! Really, who wouldn't be angry and resentful? She gets to sit around and feel sorry for herself, while everyone else has to work for what they get. If I didn't do it, nothing would ever get done around here. Even so, she still gets all the love and attention from Elkanah.

She's obsessed with not being able to have a child. She even asked the Lord for a son. She told the Lord that if he would give her a son, then she would dedicate him to the temple when he was old enough. What business does that woman have with a son? She only cares about herself! Why would any sane woman want to bear a child, raise it, and then knowingly have to give it up when he was old enough? What is the point? To my surprise, she got what she wanted. What else is new!? Nine months later she was blessed with a beautiful, healthy baby boy, Samuel.

I thought maybe he would turn her life around. Wrong! I believe it made her worse. She still had her nasty attitude and good-for-nothing lifestyle. She wanted to be waited on hand and foot, 24/7. All she wanted to do was to pamper herself.

As for Samuel: Oh Samuel, I love that boy. I raised him, you know? Yep! Just like one of my very own! He is mine, I tell you, mine! I may not have given birth to him, but that is the only thing I didn't do. I coaxed him out of his mother, and fed him like one of my own. (Hannah didn't want her breasts to sag.) He was such a joy as a child. He was so sweet, and kind to everyone. But she got all the credit. Not me! Nope! Not ever!

When we went to give him to the Lord, I was enraged at the way Hannah acted. She played her part very well. She acted like it was the hardest thing she ever had to do, with tears and everything. Give me a break; she didn't care. She didn't even raise the boy, I did! It was hard for me to let him go, but I knew he would make me proud. Every year, I would make him a coat and we would go to see him. Hannah insisted that she give him the coat, and since she is his "mother" I let her; I didn't want to hear her mouth, and I didn't care really, just as long as I got to see my Samuel. I'm so proud of the man he has become.

As for now, well, things aren't much different for me. I'm still the housekeeper, the maid, and the slave. Hannah is still a deadbeat, but everyone thinks she is God's gift to earth. She had more children after Samuel, and of course I looked after all of them, just as I did Samuel. It was a joy really; I loved them all. And so I have become accustomed to my life. There isn't much I can do about it, other than tell people the truth about me. *My story!*

So, if I am viewed as mean and nagging for standing up for myself and getting the credit for what I have done, then so be it! I will not be silent anymore.

BATHSHEBA

De'Anna Daniels

After the disastrous period of the Judges, Israel begged God for a king. God gave his special blessing to Israel's second king, David. As with many men in politics (even those with God on their side), David's power—combined with his libido—eventually became his downfall, causing suffering to himself and others, including Bathsheba and Uriah (2 Samuel 11–12; also 1 Kings 1–2 and Psalm 51).

HI, I'M GLAD YOU came; most people wouldn't. You would think that for one of the juiciest stories around people would come for miles to hear about it. (Nervous laugh.) I guess not. Anyway, just so you know, I've heard the rumors; I've seen the looks. I'm not completely oblivious. They call me "slut," "whore," "wench" . . . even "Jezebel." I do not belong grouped with the likes of her, I'm just sayin'.

Besides the names, there are some severe accusations. Adulterer, to start it off. It seems as if everybody and they momma thinks I tempted David. That is not the case. I remember it like it was yesterday. After my monthly cycle I had to complete the last step by taking a ceremonial bath. My maid and I went outside and she said the blessing; the bath happens every month like clockwork. Nothing out of the ordinary—garden, strip, bathe, blessing, dry, and sleep. Except, there's this loud banging at the door. My maid rushes to answer it, and it's none other than the king's guards. Fear jumps in my heart. I just know they're here to tell me that Uriah is dead. So I began to brace myself for the inevitable—he is a warrior, and I did say my last goodbyes to him months ago. The goons at the gate are saying, "Get dressed! The king needs you immediately." Well why would the king want me? I know my family worked for him and all, but why me?

Since the guards were so impatient, I dressed and left. So here's the juicy part: I was invited into a harem full of the most beautiful women around. I was rebathed and oiled; I felt like I was being pickled. The women said I was ready; then I was led away to David's chambers. We all know what happened next. I just lay there and it happened. No words were exchanged by either of us. Once he had done his business, he sent me home. He didn't even have the decency to kick me out himself. Now does that sound like I had to play the part of a temptress? This supposedly romantic escapade skipped all the romance. It was sex, and it was over.

Ushered out of the palace at night, I cried for hours. What if someone told? What if my husband found out? Too late to try and hide it; I was "with child." Here's the dilemma: David—king; husband—warrior who had been gone for some months now; me—baby. All of that equals me—stoned to death by the same people I went to the market with.

So, I did what I could. I sent David a letter. Not knowing what was going on, I had one of my maids go near the palace every day, 'cause there is always gossip being shared around the gates. She came back with news of Uriah being home. What was he home for? What plan did David have? I wasn't hearing anything and I was beginning to become furious. For all I knew, David was off telling Uriah that I had been lying with various men around Jerusalem, trying to save his honor . . . He was, after all, "the man after God's own heart." So what did I do? I cooked all of Uriah's favorites, prepared the house, and put on my most luxurious robes and gowns. I would show him I was worth keeping; he would forgive me. After all, he was my husband.

Well, needless to say, I never saw Uriah again, until his funeral. I mourned, and cried. God, I loved that man. We followed all the rituals; he had a very pleasant burial, fit for a hero. Then that darn knocking came again. The palace guards packed up my stuff and shipped me to the harem, and I became queen. David's wife. Amidst all of this, my baby boy was near birth, and the whispers around the palace foretold of my baby dying. Why? What did this beautiful baby do? I didn't believe a word; I held my head high and awaited the birth of *my* son. The closer the date was to have him, the more the rumors sped up, now with an accompanying story: David killed Uriah. Why!? Was he trying to protect me from Uriah's anger? Or was he covering for himself? (Of course he would do that.) This was an outrage. Why did this happen to me? Before my mind could even formulate a response my beautiful baby boy was born, and he was sick. Y'all know about how David pled with God for our son. What you don't know was how *I* pled. *I* screamed, *I* yelled, *I* sang, *I* cried. I did all I could; it didn't matter 'cause my son still died.

Let's recap: David uses and rapes me, kills my husband, lies about it, and who gets punished? Me and *my* son. Him sacrificed, and me punished for all time with my name full of blame (that is, if I get a name at all instead of just "Uriah's wife"). Meanwhile David goes down as one of the greatest kings in Western history. Let me tell you, he was lousy; *he* was the whore, the Jezebel. I *tempted* him? Ha!

Hell yeah, I may have ended up as queen, and I made sure my next son Solomon became king, but I struggled. I went through so much pain at the hands of that man. I deserved all the power I got. I was the noble one—you know—forgiving, forgetting, all that jazz. So now you know the story. Maybe you won't be so quick to call me a slut, or a whore . . . Give the title to someone else who deserves it. I am Bathsheba. Better yet, call me Queen Bathsheba.

JEZEBEL

Celecia Manning

During the eighth century B.C.E., the king of Canaan sought peace by offering his daughter Jezebel to Ahab, the king of Israel. Jezebel had a mind of her own, though, and became infamous for her independence and authority (1 Kings 16 to 2 Kings 9).

I GOOGLED MY NAME the other day and I was very distraught about what I saw: porn sites, lingerie, and nudity. I just can't understand why sexuality pops into people's minds when they think of me. I stared at the screen with disbelief. How dare people pass judgment on me when they don't know who I am and what I stand for? Why don't they mention how I showed resistance and stayed true to my god, Baal? Why don't they mention how I tried to stand up and save my people and my religion? Instead, they try to hold me down and slander me by calling me names like "whore" and "slut." These names do not represent me. Let me tell you who I am.

I, Queen Jezebel, am a Canaanite woman who honors the deities of my native land. As a princess, my father raised me to be strong and powerful. He taught me to stay true to my religion and to serve Baal. This has been drilled into my head from the time I was a child and has become my purpose in life. When I was young, the Israelites invaded our land and were trying to force their religion and customs upon my people. They walked

71

around saying that their god had chosen our land for *them*. Who do they think they are, invading our land and claiming it to be theirs?

As faithful followers of Baal, my father and I had devised a plan to save my religion and my people. He told me that I, as his daughter, was the only hope because only a female could fulfill this task. He asked me to be his eyes and ears and sent me to the Israelite court, betrothed to King Omri's son, Ahab. The plan worked out perfectly and I married Ahab when he became king. But he was a weak-minded bastard with no mind of his own; all he wanted was sex on demand. Without my experience in ruling and power he wouldn't have been able to watch over a country of even ten people. I easily converted him to my religion and instructed him to build altars for Baal. My people were so proud! They saw me as a savior helping to restore our ancestors' ancient religion.

But, there was one person in the way: that horrible man by the name of Elijah. He called himself a prophet; he said I was the one to blame for the drought of the land. He also blamed me for killing his god's prophets, but I had to kill them; their talk was destroying the peace and stability of our nation. So Elijah challenged my god, and after he won with his magic tricks, he killed all of my prophets! What a hypocrite! I tried to stop him, but he disappeared like he always did. I went into deep mourning for the loss of those wise men who had served my Baal so faithfully.

Another thing that seemed to get me into trouble was Naboth's vineyard. Have you put yourself in my shoes? My husband was in the house starving himself, pulling his hair, stressed out. He looked so pathetic; I couldn't stand to see him in that state. When I asked him what was the matter, he told me that Naboth, our neighbor, had refused to sell the vineyard next to the palace—we needed the space for a vegetable garden. Can you believe it? Ahab offered to give him a hefty price or a bigger, better vineyard in exchange, but Naboth proudly used his "ancestral land right" as an excuse, no doubt encouraged by Elijah. I was so angry: first at Naboth for being so insolent, and second at Ahab for being such a pushover. I was raised in a house of royalty; it was not right to disobey the king. Naboth deserved to be punished! I used Ahab's name to order Naboth's execution, and we got the vineyard. Word came to me later that Elijah had cursed Ahab to his face, and like a child Ahab went back into a sulk.

For some reason the Israelites just did not see things the way I did; they thought of me as evil and wicked. They made up horrible lies in order to deny my credibility because I was a woman standing up for my people. They wanted to get rid of me. When Jehu illegally appointed himself king of Israel, he rode with a great army and killed my son, the legitimate heir to the throne. They left him to rot in Naboth's vineyard. I was enraged! They were ruining what I had worked all my life to establish. I knew that Jehu was coming next to take my life. When he marched on the palace, I did my makeup and dressed in my finest clothes to await death. If I was going to die, at least it was for the sake of my Baal; that I would do with pride. They killed me and left my corpse for the dogs to eat. Unlike Bathsheba, who ruled from a place of weakness and resentment, I ruled with power and faithfulness.

My name is Jezebel. I am a queen.

GOD'S WIFE

Meredith Brown

Israel and Judah—or Oholah and Oholibah, derogatory names assigned to the two nations and a play on words in Hebrew—are often treated by the Hebrew prophets metaphorically as the wives of God. In these sometimes harsh writings, a wife's unfaithfulness (the pursuit of gods other than Yahweh, or pursuit of political/military alliance with other nations) is an opportunity for her jealous husband to demonstrate his own faithfulness—but not without severely punishing her first. The following piece, written in two voices, draws inspiration from several prophetic texts, including Ezekiel, Hosea, Lamentations, and Jeremiah.

> *I remember the devotion of your youth,*
>   *how as a bride you loved me*
> *and followed me through the wilderness,*
>   *through a land not sown.*

I was young when we first met—too young to be talking to men like him. He took one look at my dirty cutoffs and naturally dreaded hair and saw all the ways he could mold me into something sophisticated. I wanted nothing more than for him to tame me like that—I smelled like the stale, home-rolled cigarettes my cracked-out parents chain-smoked, and I acted tough and wild, but inside I was lonelier than a lynx.

I started spending time with him every afternoon. My parents didn't ask where I went after school, didn't seem to notice the new silky shirts, the rouge, the cheap golden globes glistening off my earlobes, and I didn't see why I should explain things to them. They didn't even meet him until the day of our wedding— he showed up at my house in his pinstripe suit, took one look at the trailer trash dump, and told me, "You can't just keep living here, Holi babe, kicking around in your own blood." So we went to the courthouse and made it all official.

In his vows he talked about the promise we were making to each other—that I would depend on him, that he would provide for and protect me, that I would never leave. In return he asked for submission and loyalty. The judge didn't ask if I had anything to say to his requirements, so I kept quiet. I lied when he asked me my age.

He slipped a purple plastic ring around my finger that night once we arrived at his sandstone apartment building. I sipped a glass of chocolate milk intensely, my eyes round as the full moon that glistened outside the window. Later as he penetrated me the first time, I bled but choked back my pain. He pushed hard and moved fast, but I found I couldn't speak or resist; I was paralyzed under the sheer magnitude of him. I couldn't afford to make him angry, now that he'd saved me from that depressing desert of family.

In the clammy sheets of our twin bed he whispered that he was all I would ever need, that he had chosen me, that we had made a covenant. I tried hard to smile, my stomach twisting into pretzel knots, and asked, "But what about friends?"

He stopped touching my back and frowned. "I am your friend."

"What about family?"

"I am your family. I'm everything and everyone you'll ever need or want, Oholibah. I have led you up out of your miserable past and given you a perfect love."

> *For the LORD your God is a consuming fire,*
> *a jealous God.*

He didn't want me to work or have outdoor activities. He said I wouldn't ever need to leave the apartment for anything. I sat and watched TV for days, for weeks.

A month in, my spine burst into flames of anxiety. The fire licked up the sides of my neck and I grew hot and shaky, unsure of how to exist when he was away at work, when I couldn't see his lips mouthing corrections to me, without his hand on the small of my back guiding me from room to room, without his fingers wrapping around my neck when I burned dinner. I started praying to a picture of him that hung above the kitchen sink, scrambling for direction, some control. I was lonelier than ever before, and growing increasingly unhappy, but I didn't want to make him feel inadequate; I didn't want to hurt him, this man who had saved me, who had brought me to an apartment overflowing with comfort, with food . . .

I stopped getting out of bed at all.

My sins have been bound into a yoke;
*   by his hands they were woven together.*
They have been hung on my neck,
*   and the Lord has sapped my strength.*

One day the phone rang, and a woman's voice sang through to me. Her name was Asherah, and she said she had just moved into the apartment next door. "I'm thinking of having a few people over later in the afternoon for a housewarming party, and the landlord said you don't go out much," she offered in a husky, warm voice. "Why don't you join us?"

I could feel the blood circulating through my body again as she spoke, melting through a light layer of my despair. "Oh, I couldn't," I heard myself say to her. "I'm pretty busy over here."

She chuckled. "Busy with what? Just come over for a few minutes. It'd be great to meet my new neighbor."

I paused, mulling over the way his dark eyes glistened with fury the one time I went out for a walk while he was at work, lost track of time, and didn't make it home until after he'd arrived. It was the first time he had hit me. He said he had to—he was a jealous husband, and needed to teach me how to be the right kind of wife. I brought this kind of punishment on myself, he told me, every time I acted like I could live without him.

"Ok, I'll come," I squeaked out, my fingers twisting the phone cord into tight knots.

The party was a blur. As soon as I walked in I fell in love with her—her chestnut hair was chopped pixie short, and she had these square-rimmed glasses that framed two big, grasshopper-green eyes. She was standing on a lion rug in the entryway holding flowers in her right hand, her gaze boring into me like an x-ray, and she was a goddess to me. I had never looked at a woman this way, but I couldn't help it with Asherah—I immediately wanted to be closer to her, to let her help me the way I knew she could, to give me the satisfaction I was lacking from my marriage, from my life.

She cornered me by the punch bowl during the party and asked me about books I'd read in school, what I was passionate about, where I wanted to travel in the future. He had never asked me anything like that—he thought that since I came from a trailer park I didn't think.

Our affair began the next day, when she stopped by after lunchtime to borrow a hammer. When she moved in to kiss me I couldn't stop her. She was too holy for me to touch back; I just let her move her hands down my sides, under my shirt, under my bra; she fondled me, I moaned with relief, I couldn't breathe . . . For months we continued this, our midafternoon explorations. I started to wake up early in the morning and would stretch for hours in pleasure. I took down the picture of him over the sink. I cooked and cleaned and read while I waited for Asherah, and at night I dreamt of her eyes burning through buildings, a bundle of lilies in one hand, a golden snake wrapped around her wrist . . .

Lady Parts

I stopped believing him when he told me I was stupid, stopped listening when he made his misguided assertions about me cheating on him with other men while he worked. Sometimes he still hit me, but I made my face harder than stone and refused to break—in my newfound autonomy I was finding hope.

> *A cry is heard on the barren heights,*
> *the weeping and pleading of the people of Israel,*
> *because they have perverted their ways.*

> *In the day of the LORD's wrath,*
> *no one escaped or survived.*

The secret dream that Asherah and I were living snapped in half on a Tuesday, when he found a love letter she had written under my pillow. I cringed as he read every word aloud . . .

Oholibah,

Why have we settled for surroundings
so inadequate?
We could push harder on the yellowing
bruise
we could open ourselves wider –
pull apart the lips of the matter and
make love to life with urgency
stare straight into the
wet cavern and proclaim
I want you, I want
your moist mysteries
your flattened nose your
farmer's tan and
the curly copper strands that
whisker out of you when
you're beneath me,
I want all that, Oholibah,
and I'll try my hardest not to
stop.

Ash

His body went rigid as he came to the name at the bottom. "Who's Ash? Who wrote this, Oholibah?" he inquired, his tone heating the room. "After all I have done for you, you've gone and fooled around, haven't you? Just like a cat in heat. You whore!"

I frantically shook my head no, tried to speak, to explain that there was no other man, but he moved toward me too quickly. In a matter of seconds he had torn my clothes off—they fluttered to the floor like leaves off a vine—and he screamed about the filthiness in my skirts. Then he punched my ribs with all his force.

"I'll find the men you've been spreading yourself out with, under every single tree, Oholibah, and I'll bring them here so you can have them all at once." He spat at me as my ribs cracked under his knuckles. "You'd like that, wouldn't you?"

> *I will gather them against you and strip you in front of them.*
> *I will bring on you the blood vengeance of my wrath and jealous anger.*
> *I will deliver you into the hands of your lovers, and they will tear down your mounds and destroy your lofty shrines.*
> *They will strip you of your clothes and take your fine jewelry.*
> *They will bring a mob against you, who will stone you and hack you to pieces with their swords. I will put a stop to your prostitution.*

Hot tears streamed down my face as he ripped out small chunks of my hair and slapped my face back and forth . . . back and forth. I blacked out.

When I came to, he was crouched down next to me, with a warm washcloth pressed to my open wounds. I looked up hesitantly at him, searching for any ashy remains of his fury-fire.

"I'm sorry that I hurt you, Oholibah," he murmured to me. "You just have to change your ways, and it will all go back to normal. I'll love you again and you'll be faithful, and it will all work out just fine, ok?"

"Ok," I whispered. "I'll do better. I'll stay."

For where can I go from your Spirit?
Where can I flee from your presence?
I will come trembling to the LORD, and beg forgiveness
his anger will subside
and peace will be restored
for a time.

PART II

Women in the Deuterocanonical Books

ANNA

Jane S. Webster

A Deuterocanonical book (found in Catholic and Orthodox Christian Bibles) tells the story of Tobit, a faithful and wise Israelite who was exiled to Nineveh by the Assyrians. Although the narrative setting is the eighth century B.C.E., this moral tale was likely written much later (in the third century B.C.E.) to instruct Jewish families how to live outside of Judea.

I AM SO HAPPY to be at home where I have all the things I need to make our lives comfortable. I have my big washtub to clean my fleece. I have my strong spinning wheel that slides so smoothly through its tracks and hums a warm sweet melody. I have my loom with the holes large enough to take the warp threads; the stone weights are just the right size to keep the threads tight. I have my favorite shuttlecock to send the weft thread from side to side. I love my garden with its barley, millet, peas, and beans; the olive and date palms bring flavor to my table. I have my comfortable clay jar with wide strong wood handles; it keeps the water cool in the heat of the day. I have my grinding stone that fits the calluses of my hands as though hands and stone were designed for each other. I have the burnt brick oven that cooks my bread. I have my warm wool shawl to keep out the winter wind. I have a bed that has molded to my old bones and cradles me to sleep. I am happy to be at home where I need only a few steps to move about from place to place. It has taken me a long time to get my home the way I want it to be.

I have not always been so settled. In the early days, after Tobit and I were first married, we used to travel to Jerusalem every Passover to take our sacrifice—the very best of all our grain, wine, olive oil, pomegranates, figs, and the best of our flocks—as a gift to the priests. Every year, he would take all the money we had saved and spend it in the city. (He said he gave it to the poor, but I wonder now.) The journey was arduous as we went from our home in Kadesh Napthali near the Sea of Galilee, along the Jordan River, and up the mountain to the Holy City. We traveled alone, as none of our family or neighbors would go with us—they worshiped in the shrines of the calf near our home instead. Tobit was proud of this constant traveling, but I found it unbearable. For three years in a row, we made the journey when I was in the first months of pregnancy, and for three years in a row, I miscarried along the way. "Never mind," said Tobit, "We can still make the sacrifice on time." He was oblivious of the pain I had, and the constant cramping in my low back, and the incessant bleeding. I focused on placing one step down after another, for five days; if I held myself in just the right way, I could keep the wincing to a minimum. (Tobit became so intolerant of my gasps.) Once we arrived in Jerusalem, I would lie in the tent with hot stones on my abdomen, trying to regain my strength before it was time to make the long trek back. When we returned home from the pilgrimage, I would count the days until we would have to leave again.

After we had been married about six years, I was seven months pregnant when Passover approached, and I feared that I would miscarry again; Tobit reluctantly gave me permission to stay at home. For the first time I was able to keep the weeds from overtaking my garden and protect the young lambs from the wolves. I experimented with wool and dyes and made beautiful fabrics, and sold them in the market. My home had the luxury of

84

unbroken attention. And I had my first and only son, Tobias. I vowed that I would teach him to be gentle with his wife.

When Tobias was three and I was about three months along with another, Tobit again went to Jerusalem for the sacrifice. While he was gone, the Assyrians attacked our city and destroyed our home. They smashed our jugs, broke my loom and the baby's cradle, ate all of the sheep (even the new lambs), and burned our house down. They took everything. I tried to hide with Tobias in a cave but they found us and chained us to the others and forced marched us to Nineveh, their capital city. It took more than a year to get there. I had to carry Tobias most of the way; he was so small and weak from lack of food and water. After seven months, Tobit caught up with us, but I had already buried our baby girl by the side of the road. The soldiers led us to our new home among strangers.

Because Tobit could read, write, and work with numbers, he was put in charge of accounts and all the buying and selling for the king. He loved it, for after a time he got to travel far and wide to bring back exotic fabrics, jewels, spices, and seeds. Once he traveled to Media, and thinking he needed to protect his growing wealth, he left about twenty talents (about seven hundred pounds) of silver with his cousin Gabael in Rages. When he was home, he would brag about his journeys and give gifts to the other Israelites who lived in the city. He especially liked to boast about "burying the bodies" of the men that the king put to death; he said it was to honor their bodies, but I think he was getting to their purses before Shalmaneser could. Once the king heard that Tobit was stealing from him, he tried to arrest him, but Tobit ran away and hid. The soldiers again came and took everything we had. My young son and I were left bleeding, shamed, and with only rags to cover our torn flesh.

We managed as best as we could. I did the wash for some women in the city (women who earned their living on their backs); I wove their cloth and ground their meal; my son carried wood for their fires and lugged their water jugs; they shared their food with us. They were sweet to us, especially to Tobias, but I did not join them in their work. My body was too old and dried up for that.

After a month, Tobit showed up again full of excitement; his nephew had been given a good job in the government and had put in a good word. (Shalmaneser had died and his son now ruled.) As quickly as our fortunes had disappeared, they returned. We rebuilt our old house and I worked hard to put it all in order again. I prepared a feast and just as everything was ready, Tobit, ever trying to prove his righteousness, sent our son out to look for some poor people who might come in to share our meal and honor him. We waited as the delicious food grew cold and stale.

An hour later, Tobias returned home wide-eyed and fearful; he had witnessed a gang of soldiers murder a traveler from Persia! The body was lying outside our courtyard. Tobit leapt up, found the body, sifted through his possessions, then quickly buried him before anyone would see. I couldn't believe it! I cried, "How could you put your family at risk again by doing such a thing! Shame on you!" I pushed him out of the house. I was so disgusted, even more so as I watched him wander down the road to the house of women.

The next day, Tobit showed up at the gate with painful eyes. He said that the birds had shit in his eyes, but I was more inclined to think that he had been infected by one of the women. We spent all we had on physicians, but Tobit eventually lost his sight. He begged his cousin to help us, and we went through all his money as well. If only Tobit had stayed home, we would have been all right.

Now I had to earn the living for our family. I began to gather the wool fragments caught in the fences and along the city walls. I cleaned, spun, and wove, and bit by bit I was able to buy better wool. People liked my fabrics, dyes, and patterns—based on the traditional designs of the Galilean people—and they began to commission more and more pieces. One woman liked my work so much that she gave me a bonus of a small goat! I felt so proud and excited—it had been such a long time since we had enjoyed some meat. But when I got the goat home, Tobit heard it bleat and accused me of stealing it. Stealing it! I was so angry! He was the thief, not me! He was the one who had brought all this hardship on us! Tobit was so insulted by my accusations that he began to pray for death, talking about suicide. I considered helping him; he had caused us so much trouble and claimed to be so righteous! But if Tobit killed himself, our neighbors would think us cursed and turn us out; our life would be even harder.

Then a few days later, Tobit suddenly decided to send our son Tobias on a journey to get the treasure he had stashed in Media, in order, he said, "to give us both a proper burial." My whole world started to spin. Was my son to take up his father's practices and travel around the world, leaving me exposed to calamity? Travel was so dangerous: people were often kidnapped, murdered, or robbed. Surely, an immature, inexperienced boy would fall prey to treachery. My heart broke. Not only would I have to deal with my husband by myself, I would have to do it without the solace and support of my son. I wished I were dead.

Tobit would not back down despite my objections. He sent our son out to find a guide who would take him to Rages, and to my surprise Tobias returned with a tall, handsome Israelite named Azariah who was somehow related to us. Azariah had been to Media many times, a fact that gave me some small comfort. (I only wished that he was bigger and stronger!)

I figured that the round trip from Nineveh to Rages would take two to three months. After two months had passed, I began to watch for Tobias and his guide. At first, I passed the time by stitching garments as I sat by the door. Eventually, I could no longer see through the tears. I moved up to the city wall so that I could watch the road. Day after day, I took up my post straining my weakened eyes to see far into the distance. Day after day, Tobit complained that I left him alone and unattended. After four months, I had given up hope of ever seeing my son again. Surely he was dead by the side of the road. But I continued to climb up to the city wall out of habit. My knees and back ached; my skin flushed with desperate heat; my breath grew raspy. But I enjoyed the peaceful separation from my needy and demanding husband.

In the sixth month, I watched with dead eyes as a caravan of camels approached the city. As they came closer and closer, I saw that a little dog was running with them—our dog! My son was coming home! I scrambled down the wall and out the gate and ran to meet them. Tobias, so strong and tall now, caught me up in his arms and I burst into tears! He laughed. I didn't know whether to embrace him or to shake him. Relief washed over me.

In the end, we were fully restored. Tobias, bless him, brought back a healing medicine for Tobit's eyes, a wonderful wife Sarah, and great wealth from his new father-in-law. We made room for the newlyweds and then, eventually, to my great joy, their seven sons and nine daughters, one of whom they named after me—Little Anna. They would climb into my lap and stroke my wrinkled face in wonder and delight.

My husband no longer travels or looks for bodies in the city; thankfully, he keeps to himself and studies his books. He no longer comes to my bed. My son has taught him to be more considerate. The children surround me and I watch as their little fingers become deft and strong with the spinning wheel, the loom, the grinding stone, and the garden. The women in my city pay me well for my fabrics, and every month I put some money aside to use as I wish. At night, when I retreat to the comfort of my single bed and surround my old body with warm blankets that smell of sunshine, I no longer have need of dreams. I am content.

Judith's Slave

Lizy Velazquez

The Deuterocanonical book of Judith, chapters 8–16, recounts the terror experienced by Bethulia, a small Israelite city under siege by Assyrian troops. They have been given an ultimatum: surrender or die. When the city elders decide to surrender, Judith steps forward to save the day. Or does she?

My name is Shua, meaning "The Forgotten One." When my owner Judith calls me, she doesn't call me by my name. She says, "Hey you, slave! Come here." I hate her; she has ruined my life. You see, I do everything for her, even think for her. But to her I am just a slave.

She came home one day begging me to help her get away from Bethulia before it fell to Holofernes, the Assyrians' powerful army leader. Holofernes and his army were known to be invincible—and ruthless. They had cut off the water supply to the city; if it did not rain and alleviate the drought, Bethulia would have to surrender in five days. Our people were starting to think that it would be better to be taken as slaves by Holofernes than to die of thirst. But Judith knew what happened to beautiful victims of war. So, fearing to find herself enslaved, she told me that she would give me my freedom if I would help her. It came as no great surprise that she asked for my help. Although she has the beauty, and the money, she definitely doesn't have the brains or the guts. She even lacks the determination to resort to devious means to get what she wants. Well of course, I accepted; having my freedom back was all I ever thought about.

I had once known what freedom was. When I was still young, my parents gave me to Judith to pay off their debt to her. Each year she gave me more and more responsibility, and now, especially since her husband died, I run her estate. Because Judith has not paid me for what I do, I have no way to earn back my freedom. She won't even allow me to marry a fellow slave; she says a family would be too distracting and she needs me full-time. I longed to be free and to have a family, so I willingly agreed to help.

I devised a plan—brilliantly simple, if I do say so myself—to use Judith to seduce Holofernes. Then we would kill him, and she would set me free.

First, Judith needed to tell the elders not to do anything rash because "she" had a plan to save Bethulia: I went to call them. I was really nervous, but they agreed to come. She told them, as I had instructed, that she was going to do something to stop Holofernes. Uzziah, one of the elders, basically told her to pray and leave everything as it was. But Judith refused, and told the elders we would be leaving Bethulia that night. They actually praised her for her wisdom and courage! I gathered together a bag of food and our dishes. I got her clothes out, the ones she used to wear when her husband was living. I helped her to get dressed and to put on all her jewelry. I rather enjoyed prettying her up for some man to objectify and use, the way she had objectified and used me.

We left Bethulia and were swiftly captured by the Assyrian patrol. They questioned us about where we were from. I whispered in Judith's ear, "Tell them we left Bethulia so we could join them to help take the city and to save ourselves." The Assyrians stupidly believed us (did I mention how beautiful Judith was?) and escorted us to Holofernes. He and the other men marveled at her, ravishing her with their eyes. At my prompting, Judith told

Holofernes the same lie she had told the patrol. She also told him that we would pray every night to get strategic information from God, to know when the Bethulians were at their weakest. Very early each morning, she bathed in the spring "to purify herself for prayer," but I encouraged her to linger into the dawn, and let her clothes slip off her shoulder. The soldiers went mad with lust.

By the fourth day, Holofernes invited Judith to a private banquet, just as we had hoped. As I massaged scented oil into her body, attached her jewelry, adjusted her clothes, and fixed her hair, I laid out the plan for her. I told Judith to avoid the Assyrians' food and drink, but to keep filling Holofernes' cup. (I added salt to his food to encourage his thirst.) I told her to flatter and flirt with him. As we expected, Holofernes took Judith to his bedchamber. I waited outside, listening for the time to act. When I heard his snores, I slipped into the room. Judith was praying, tears running down her cheeks. Before I let myself feel any sympathy for her, I quickly grabbed the sword above the bed and thrust it into her hands.

But Judith was so weak she couldn't go through with the plan! Perhaps she finally understood what it meant to be a pawn in someone else's plans, or perhaps she was just drunk. Either way she seemed to have lost her nerve. I didn't waste any time. I took the sword from her and slashed his neck once. Stunned, he opened his eyes and his body trembled; the look in his eyes said he understood in an instant what it meant to be ravished. With a second blow, I slashed his head the rest of the way off. He stopped moving. I grabbed Holofernes' head and slipped it into our food bag. Judith just stood there gaping. She started to shake and cry and talk all at once. "Silence," I told her.

I took her by the hand and led her, like a child, out of the tent and toward the spring. The guards let us pass as usual because they thought we were going to pray. When they could no longer see us in the dark, we changed direction and went up the hill to Bethulia.

When we went through the city gates, Judith was still speechless so I told everyone what "she" had done. Everyone surrounded her as she stood with the head of Holofernes, as if it were a trophy. Even the high priest Joakim came to witness what she had done and blessed her. All of this was fine with me, until we were in private again and she came back to herself. She said I wouldn't be free until the day she died; she "needed me too much." She couldn't live without me, her loyal slave. Perhaps my plan worked too well. After all I had risked to have my freedom and my own family, I got nothing.

Yes, Judith is a liar. Surprised? Because she is rich, because she is beautiful, you all believed her. You thought she was the one who was courageous, when in fact she was too childish to come up with a plan, too afraid to face Holofernes by herself. You believed she could, because you wanted to believe her. But because I am a nameless slave in your stories, a nobody, you didn't even notice me.

My name says it all: Shua, "The Forgotten One."

SUSANNA

Jamie A. Smith

The story of Susanna and the Elders, one of three additions to the book of Daniel (chapter 13), is considered apocryphal by Protestant Christians but is included in both Orthodox and Roman Catholic canons. Susanna is famous for maintaining her sexual purity in the face of threats from two powerful men, and depictions of her nude form were among the most popular images of biblical women in Renaissance art.

SUSANNA MADE IT INTO the Bible the way most women do—on account of what did or did not happen to her vagina. That's me—her vagina. You've probably not heard of us unless you are familiar with Renaissance paintings, but I'll get to that in a minute. You see, in the holiest of holy books, women are usually vessels through which men prove their virtue or prowess, or women are canvases upon which men perform their masculinity. Which is to say, women don't make it into the story unless it helps to further the plot for the men. They appear only as the larger incarnation of their reproductive organs. (Can you think of a woman with a name who made it into the story when her vagina wasn't her *raison d'etre*? Wives are in the Bible because their vaginas give their husbands babies. Daughters are in there so that fathers can show off protecting their vaginas. Oh, there are some rebellious midwives, but they work with vaginas, so it's still a vagina-focused show. And don't go throwing Mary's vagina at me! That is the all-time vagina story: what *did not*—but then *did*—happen to her vagina. That was one for the records.)

Our story, Susanna's and mine, is quite simple, though we are by no means the main characters. It could have been any woman, really. The main point of the story is that a clever young man was so clever in his clever justice-seeking mind that he saved our life. Cleverly. So, what happened to me? In this instance, thankfully, it is a case of what didn't happen to me, but could have. Susanna was bathing us in the garden—as she did routinely when the judges left her husband's house at lunchtime to go home to their wives. Since the Jews had been scattered, it was up to the small community to govern themselves. Joakim's house served as the court. A couple of perverts—the Bible refers to them as ancient judges who were filled with Babylonian wickedness (oh, glorious euphemism)—figured out that a noon time bath was Susanna's habit so they hatched a plan to approach us while we were rather vulnerable. Now, I admit that I love a good bath. (The whole "cleanliness is next to godliness" idea—you know some vagina-loving woman came up with that.) Susanna, she liked to keep me happy. She routinely sent her servants away once she had settled in so that we could, um, approach that mystical plane. On that day, I think we were both feeling relaxed and, well, loose. However, the creepers, who were hiding in the garden, waited until the coast was clear then appeared and stated their interest. Susanna didn't have to consult me. As soon as I figured out what they were saying, I closed up like a shopkeeper on holiday. Seriously. I dried up like the desert Moses crossed.

Not that these men were the kind who would take no for an answer. Worse, they had a strategy for when she did say no (which made me think that they'd played this game before). They told her that either she would have sex with them or they would tell everyone that they saw her take a young lover. Good one, right? No one would believe she'd willingly have sex with the likes of them, but a young handsome man would be plausible. I knew my preference. I kept as closed up as I could. I got so tight that not even a grain of sand would have passed through me.

Now, I had only experienced one penis, but one was enough. As far as I'm concerned, a penis is a dangerous thing except under the right circumstances, and this was far from an advantageous situation. I knew this from Joakim's penis. The man may have meant well, but it never took a prophet to tell what kind of night we would have. If Joakim's belly protruded because he ate too much, his penis was wary, and the only chance I stood of enticing it in was if there was no work involved on his part. If Joakim came to bed amorous, but slurring a bit and repeating himself, his penis was groggy and I walked the fine line of gentle and measured provocation. If Joakim received bad news, his penis was a bully and I usually ended up bruised and bleeding. And, if Joakim stayed in the kitchen too long with the servants, his penis was asleep and nothing I did would wake it. Other times, we could generally work together. We certainly worked best when Joakim was in a good mood and not too bothered that Susanna wanted to take a few minutes to prepare for bed. That's when she would get me ready for Joakim. But, I promise you, all the preparing in the world wouldn't have made me pliable for those men.

Susanna's was a good story to pick for the moralists because she'd rather die than let anyone who wasn't her husband near me. And I would rather swim with crocodiles than have two angry penises fighting for domination. So, instead of giving in, she raised holy hell with her voice in the garden. I think they heard her clear to Jerusalem.

However, since the elders were trusted men of the community, we were accused and sentenced to death for infidelity. I remember showing up in court. We were scared. Susanna was also ashamed. I wasn't ashamed. I kept hoping that they'd ask me. Put me to the test. I could prove that no young lover had passed through. But they didn't. Instead, the clever judge I mentioned earlier stepped up. (Yup, you know the formula to any good story: insert hero and mix.) He's the star. You'll know him as Daniel. We knew him as the young judge who liked to buck the system. Susanna's husband Joakim complained about him constantly. Personally, I thought the judge was cute, till he opened his mouth. After a few minutes of that, I was ready to chuck him in with the lions.

Now, don't get me wrong. I appreciate cleverness. And, I think Susanna appreciated living—at least in the moment of her vindication. But for the longest time, our story was any woman's story and we were only the vehicle for clever Daniel to prove his cleverness, which he did. He asked to question the men separately to make sure their stories matched. Well, the creeping creepers from creepsville hadn't thought that far ahead so they chose different trees under which they supposedly "knew" me. Clever. Problem solved.

Except you know that it wasn't. You don't read any more about Susanna or me in the Bible. She'd served her purpose. Daniel had been introduced to the community as a wise young elder. The Bible continues on its merry, righteous way without bothering to describe the hassle that we faced. See, once a vagina has been called out, as I had been, once a woman's virtue has been questioned, as Susanna's had been, we were tainted. For life. There was talk. People said things like, "What was she doing bathing regularly like that so that men might be tempted?" and, "They did see her naked after all." That did it for Joakim's house, too. The judges moved on to a house that did not contain the stain of misconduct, which I didn't mind. It upset Joakim, however. He didn't visit with me for weeks. Unfortunately, when he did after, he was usually aggressive with me and accusatorial towards Susanna. Those nice public words of support died in the doorway.

The worst part for me was that the incident curtailed our bath times. We both soured on those. As much as I loved being in the garden, I couldn't relax. Susanna kept looking towards the bushes and I stayed tense until we were back in the house.

Modesty prevailed even indoors, and she was all business when she bathed. As a result, I no longer received any special attention. All because some pathetic men fell in lust with her.

That is what should have been the end of our story. But no one heard it from our perspective—the Bible's not written that way. The story essentially faded from memory. Some versions of the Bible don't even include it as part of the book of Daniel, which is fine by me. I never wanted to become public property.

But the Renaissance painters, man, they brought us back. Per-verts. Christian perverts, at that. Painting achieved a higher quality and the subjects became more life-like during the Renaissance. Some male artists, anxious to paint nudes, sought out stories of nude women in the Bible that they could "legitimately" paint to further the faith: pornography turned "religious art." The paintbrush became the new sex toy. (Not all artists preferred the female form. Check out Michelangelo's women and you'll have no doubts about his orientation. But most men sought justification for painting naked women.) Hence, Susanna and I enjoyed a "rebirth'" of our popularity.

And here is where I really start to take offense. The subject of that chapter is Daniel—as I stated before. But these artists all chose to paint the one scene in which we were exposed, while Daniel is nowhere to be found! They don't depict the important moment of him questioning the judges separately. They focus on seeing us nude. Worse, it's almost as if they heard the critics from our day, and shifted the blame to Susanna. She was the temptress. After all, she was naked; I was exposed. Don't believe me? Look us up. The images are all there in living color.

The expression on her face that these artists assume for her really boils my blood. They depict everything from shock and surprise (with a little delight) to acceptance and joy. Joy. Seriously. Now, I know you might defend Guido Reni. After all, a man who painted such a loving Joseph holding his miracle baby boy could not be all bad. But have you seen his *Susanna and the Elders*? She barely looks surprised. And the "elders"? Why, they're almost handsome. They look nothing like the creeps who sneaked into our garden. Tintoretto is even worse; he has vain Susanna admiring us in a mirror like someone at a get-to-know-your-vagina workshop.

The worst offender is probably Alessandro Allori. The creeps look much closer to me in that depiction than they ever were in real life. Spectators welcome. And his Susanna looks as though she's accepting their advances and pulling them in. That's contrary to how even the Bible reported it.

I will say that there is one depiction from that time which isn't bad. You can tell from Susanna's body language just how disgusted and afraid we were. This one is by a woman, of course— Artemisia Gentileschi. There's someone who clearly knew what it was like to be a woman in a man's world. Her vagina must have talked her through that painting.

After the Renaissance, once pornography was "invented," well, our story faded back into obscurity, only to be trotted out by the industrious preacher from time to time. Yet, I do find it interesting that, with all that has changed, some things persist. Our story could still happen almost anywhere in the world today, and the result would be the same. Granted, the woman would not be condemned to death in most modern places, but she would still be blamed. I would be blamed. No amount of washing can ever remove the stain left by lies or rumors. For life. A tainted vagina is just that. Tainted.

PART III

Women in the New Testament

MARY, THE MOTHER OF JESUS

Jessica Becker Beamer

The first chapters of the Gospels according to Matthew and Luke include infancy narratives of Jesus that describe Mary from Galilee, who "conceived by the Holy Spirit" and became the mother of Jesus. According to John 19:25, Mary was also at the cross when Jesus died. For centuries, she has been celebrated by Christian churches as theotokos—the mother of God. Catholics believe Mary remained a virgin until she died; Protestants generally accept that Jesus had younger siblings (see Matthew 13:55).

VIRGIN MARY. VIRGIN BIRTH. Saint of All Saints. It sounds like I have no vagina story to share, no "woman's story" to tell. And I don't have a typical story to share, do I? But I have a story, and it's not the one that all of you try to give me.

Mine is a story of loss. Powerlessness too, but more than anything, loss. I was a good Jewish girl and knew what was expected of me. I was to marry Joseph, support him in his business, and most importantly have kids. Lots of kids, if possible, for that was how we planned for the future. I didn't ask to be revered by centuries of Christians. Obviously, when this all started I didn't even know what a Christian was. I just wanted to be loved and honored by my children. I knew what society would have me do and I agreed to do it: follow the requests of our parents and marry Joseph. And Joseph wasn't a bad catch—reliable, some solid carpentry skills, trusted by others, soft-spoken, on the older side, maybe a little bit of a pushover. I thought we'd make some beautiful babies together, and we did, eventually. But the first one was never ours to keep. As I said, mine is a story of loss.

Loss. Whoever heard of a woman who *agreed* to have God's child? I was a female and a kid myself, remember? I had no choice, no voice. It was my worst nightmare: bright interrogation lights, some kind of spirit in white, me cowering in the corner, losing control of my bladder. Terror, powerlessness, choked-back sobs. A messenger claiming to be from God told me that I was to carry and deliver a son, God's son, and the child's name would be Jesus. This messenger sweetened the conversation by calling me "highly favored." So, yes, I did say, "Lord, let it be to me as you have said," or something close to that. But what would you have said—"NO"? "No, God"? "Don't touch me"? "Choose someone else"? Young, terrified, and impressionable, I agreed. And you *praise* me for the maturity of my response in accepting the role of "Mother of God." That is the part I don't get, because, call it what you want, I was raped. Rape occurs when one person takes all of the sexual power from another person—that's rape, right? Then yes, I was raped. Rape is rape, whether by God or a human, and my vagina reminds me of that every day of my life. So, I said "Yes," but it was "Yes" born of coercion, of fear.

Loss. My vagina missed the first big event of its life. I was pregnant, yes, but all the action was in the womb. According to the angel, I was carrying an important baby boy, God's boy, and I had very little say about the whole thing. I didn't ask to be a surrogate. I didn't get to choose, not really. And that was just the first of many choices that I never got to make. Whether or not I wanted to be pregnant was never open for discussion. Unlike adultery. In adultery a choice is made. Do I want to sleep with this man? Risk pregnancy? Risk being ostracized? Is the physical pleasure worth the consequence? In rape, any choices are made under duress. All this talk over the years about "Mary, the Chosen One." God chose me. I had no real choice. Not that I'm bitter. Okay, maybe I am bitter. Loss does that to a woman.

Loss. By carrying this God-planted baby, I was dependent on Joseph's belief in my story—God's story thrust on both of us. What kept us going? A numb hope that we were indeed chosen, special, and favored; somehow great rewards would come out of this situation. As daily life replaced the aura from our bizarre angel visitations, we both had doubts about what we had seen, and what we had done. I could tell that Joseph often resented me, and this baby who was not his. But his was a quiet resentment, not a teeming anger. I really craved sex, not just the emotional connection, but the physical contact and release. As my belly grew, my appetite for sex increased as markedly as my appetite for food. I wanted Joseph and I wanted him to want me. We had no sex while I was pregnant with God's son. Joseph said he was afraid to hurt the baby. He said sex felt wrong. There were moments, though, when we managed to pretend that this was just a normal first pregnancy.

Loss. I didn't ask to be pregnant, but I did what all mothers do. I fell in love . . . with the unseen but always-moving baby. He was so strong, so solid in my belly, so real. I loved the deep groin ache that would start when I felt the power of his strong kicks. Sometimes I even felt hope and longed to raise him as my child, our child. I fantasized that he would look like us—Joseph's face, my eyes—and no one would know that he wasn't, not really. But I also wanted to believe that by being God's child he would be favored and healthier, smarter, and more loving than all other children. And he would be mine. I was a foolish woman. From the very beginning, he was never mine. My vagina knew this. My heart longed for another story.

Loss. Joseph's loss of pride and trust mirrored my own. While my vagina story is only mine, he has quite a penis story to tell, doesn't he? What kind of man starts his married life cuckolded by God? Oh, the humiliation—for both of us. History has decided that we are holy, faithful, even saints. The truth was that, especially during my pregnancy, we were ashamed. Given my pregnancy of suspicious beginnings, Joseph did have a choice, and he chose to keep me. But it wasn't easy to keep him. He spent our long married life needing to choose me over and over again. But he stayed, and I stayed.

Loss. A hellish memory of a trip to Bethlehem. Joseph still wouldn't touch me. We were barely talking. Then an excruciating birth in a filthy barn. No mother, no sister to help. Just Joseph, and he didn't know a thing about birthing. I needed human contact, any human contact. Joseph held my hand and kept slapping the animals away from where I lay on my back in the muck. Let me tell you there was no relief from pain just because this baby was the son of God. Painful, raw, explosive ripping, then . . . my son. The moment I smelled his briny sweet scent, I knew him and wanted him. He might be God's son, but he was mine too. The joyous agony of nursing him, a high like I had never felt before. Finally this was the connection I had been longing for during the past nine months of loneliness.

Loss. Jesus. An unusual name and a presumptuous one. Joseph and I had some late-night debates about whether or not we really needed to call him that. "Rescuer." It felt like a public boast. We didn't even get to choose his name.

Loss. Jesus was a lonely child even in the midst of the crowds that were always swarming around him. We didn't get to raise him as we saw fit. He just seemed to raise himself. Wandering off to temples, talking to strangers, disappearing in plain sight—a real pistol. Didn't I deserve an obedient son who would provide for his parents? Oh no, this one was the son of God. Joseph? The pain and humiliation this caused him. Me? I knew Jesus loved me, but I still felt such a large gulf between us. Jesus treated me as if I was just one of the many he loved. I had no ability to control him or tell him what to do. While he would treat me with quiet respect at times, even listen and respond to my pleas as he did in Cana, he would calmly and publicly disregard my motherly requests at other times as he pursued some task or direction known only to him. Mine was not the voice to guide him. I didn't even get to raise my son. God took that away from me too.

Loss. I'm not the first mother to lose her son. I'm not the first mother to witness her son's death. I may be the first mother to know that her son's life is a sacrifice for God's plan. This did not exactly improve my relationship with God. These were the angriest days of my life. Jesus' death seemed so senseless in my eyes, a mother's eyes.

Loss. After the crazy start to my reproductive years, I never really trusted my body. I mean, birth without human intercourse? What was my body going to do next? While Joseph was gentle, he was afraid of my body too. Sex was always . . . complicated, shameful. We never had a chance to connect as man and wife before God got involved. Trust in the normal order of things had broken down.

Loss. No matter what people think, I was not always a virgin. Joseph and I had other children, ordinary children with ordinary lives. And I loved them as a mother should love her children. Joseph loved them even more than I did, for there was never any shame attached to them. Honestly, they felt like a reward for handing over my firstborn to God. Those other births weren't easy, but they were mine. My vagina knew how these babies came to be and how they entered the world. When the oldest of these was born, for the very first time I felt powerful.

Virgin birth, Madonna, Saint of All Saints, Mother of God. They sound good on paper, but they're not my vagina story. History has given me a lot of glory and I can't say it hasn't caused me to feel pride at times. But I didn't ask for it. I wanted kids, not kings. My vagina? Written out of the story by your very words: Blessed Virgin.

BLEEDING WOMAN

Lizy Velazquez

The story of a woman with a hemorrhage appears in all three Synoptic Gospels: Matthew 9:20–22, Mark 5:25–34, and Luke 8:43–49. Her constant bleeding was most likely from her vagina, thereby rendering her ritually unclean according to Jewish law, and making her a social outcast. In each case, the unnamed woman affects her own healing by touching Jesus' cloak as he passes through a crowd; Jesus declares that her faith has made her well.

MY NAME IS CHERÁN. I am a small town in big Mexico. I am here looking for help. I am bleeding.

Many of my people have left me for a place they say is bigger and better than me and they call it "El Norte," the North, better known as the United States. She is rich, glamorous, new. She makes them promises. They leave me because I am old and spoiled and no longer clean, safe, or of value. I have become violated and defiled.

The only thing I have to offer to my people who are still here is being taken away, pulled away, and dragged away: my forest, my beautiful forest, and its trees. The trees used to give them food, shade, shelter. But now the wood that my people get from these trees is valued only because it is the thing that helps them make money. The wood is used to craft guitars that make music around the world. Now, strangers are coming to my forests and stealing the trees to sell for money, money they will not share with my people. The strangers cut down the trees and drag them through my streets. When my people try to stop the bleeding of trees, they face violence. Now their blood, too, is running down the streets. My forests are being raped, and I am hemorrhaging my most precious possession.

Help, you ask? Help costs around here. The police get paid, but they do nothing! The governor? He speaks about action but does nothing. We have no money now. We have spent all that we had. Now we are surrounded by the military, saying they will control the violence, but they are powerless in the face of greed, and blood still runs down the streets.

Now who will help us? Whose garment may I touch to stop the blood from running down? Who may I touch to make my people feel safe again? Jesus?

Jesus, just listen to me! Look at me! I am on my knees asking for help! I am reaching out with faith. I know you are on your way to heal other villages that have suffered like my people have, but please don't ignore me. Let me believe my people will be healed with a simple touch. I promise not to dirty your holy clothes with my blood, the blood of my forests, my people. Just please help me! I know this blood makes you think I am not pure, but the hearts of my people, my trees, are pure. Isn't that what really matters?

Jesus! Please! Just turn around and help me.

Samaritan Woman

Mallory Magelli

*When Jesus enters into the hostile territory of Samaria, he stops at
a well and asks a woman for a drink of water, even though it is not
appropriate for a Jewish man to speak to or drink with a Samaritan
woman (John 4:1–42). As they speak, Jesus reveals a truth about her
that leads to her conversion; the whole village also comes to believe
because of her testimony.*

IT WAS MY SECOND time going to the well that day; I remember
it clearly. I knew what people were saying about me as I passed
them on the streets. Women would stare, whisper, and snicker.
They called me a tramp and a whore, but they did not know the
truth; their judgments were something they had created from
nothing.

The truth was that I once had five husbands; each of them
died on our wedding night, killed by a demon. The young men
stopped fighting for me—or their fathers had stopped them.
Then I was left without children. My vagina had never been
entered; my womb had never been swollen with child. My skirt
hung loosely from my narrow hips. That alone set me apart from
the other women. They thought my curse would rub off on them,
so they all stayed away. They told me I needed a man, so I invited
a friend to live with me, one who never bothered me—his eyes

were elsewhere, and he was rarely home. The other women assumed he was my husband.

I loved going to the well in the quiet of midday when the sun was its hottest; it was an act of worship for me. As a woman, I was not permitted to study in any capacity, but when I went to the well and performed my rituals, I spent time listening and being alone with my God. As I felt the coolness of the water, and tasted its sweetness, I imagined that I was drinking in God and drawing healing into my soul. Because of the experiences I had at the well, I was filled with some sort of powerful spirit. With this power, I was able to overcome the obstacles placed before me: I could look after myself; I had the strength and courage to worship and provide for myself in a way no other human could; I needed no man.

But that day, when I approached the well, a man was sitting there, and he asked me for a drink of water. Of course, I was skeptical at first, knowing Jewish men looked down on anyone from Samaria, especially women; he did not know the power that I enjoyed. I was not very inviting, for he had interrupted me during my daily ritual. He told me his name was Jesus and I was stunned when he claimed to be better than my ancestor Jacob. He talked about this living water that would never leave me thirsty: it would free me from my chains of continually coming to the well to draw water twice a day and give me a new way to worship away from the well.

I needed time to process this. There were two opposing emotions for my heart and head to filter. On the one hand, I could do my work in the city uninterrupted; I would not have to trek to the well, so would have fewer aches and pains. On the other hand, I refused to become dependent on this man for water. After my experiences with men, I knew that I didn't need him because I was able to take care of myself. I told Jesus so and he was taken aback, but responded that his water would be a gift to me for all of my work; he needed *me* in order to make his water known through worship. It turned out that I already knew what Jesus was saying through my mystical experience with God at the well, but he challenged me to share it with the rest of my community, to step out and share my experiences.

Much to my surprise, the more I shared with my neighbors, the more they responded; they too began to understand and worship with the living water. They also began to see me for who I really was. They learned my story and understood my hardships. As their compassion for my suffering grew, they began to be aware of others who suffered: so many people who line our streets and fill our homes suffer in ways that cry out for healing, love, compassion, and understanding. My neighbors now see those who are hungry, hurt, and humiliated. My town and the families of my past husbands now understand that the demon did not live within me; they know their judgments were unfair, unjust, and untimely. Now they see me—not as a woman without a husband, but as one empowered by the Spirit, as one who knows God and true worship. They too drink the living water and are free, bringing freedom and justice to others.

WOMAN CAUGHT IN ADULTERY

Lisa Nichols Hickman

A much-beloved story of a nameless woman caught in adultery appears only in the Gospel according to John (chapter 8). As a Jewish crowd gathers to stone her for her sin, as commanded in God's law, Jesus merely writes in the sand. When he finally declares that the person who is without sin should be the one to cast the first stone, the crowd disperses. Neither they nor Jesus see fit to condemn her.

STONES ARE FORMED BY pressure, time, and heat.

I know a lot about all three.

The pressure of a man. Time for mistakes. Heat. Mistakes repeated. You see, I needed to be needed. Desperately.

I can tell you about the heat of the moment. That's where they found me, in the very act—speechless and undressed. Both of us were guilty, but they let him remain.

Stones are hard-pressed. They certainly don't speak but their surfaces tell stories. The fissures and deposits are an aggregation of all the stone has experienced.

My words, my voice, are buried under the layers of my life.

Over time, those words have been pushed down. Pushed from lip to throat, throat to chest, chest to heart, heart to belly, belly to womb. Womb to . . . well, my words are here now. They've traveled from lip to lip.

Even without speaking, that Jesus had a voice.

Lady Parts

Surrounding me was the invective of armed and angry men. I felt their words pelt every cell in my body. But that Jesus assumed a different stance.

How could he have such confidence to surrender his word to the gesture of his flesh?

Stooped to the knee, sand at his feet, he touched his finger to the ground. Energy from heaven to temple to ground pulsated at his very fingertips. He didn't speak and yet he spoke volumes as the circle around him leaned in.

I grew angry as he paused. According to the law, my life was just moments from ending. I could practically feel the stones pounding my flesh, my bones.

As his finger moved, I wondered what he would write. My name? A sacred text? A list of sins? The men I've known? The law that demands: stone her?

His hand, so gentle. So unlike the hands of other men I knew. I always studied the lines on their hands because I couldn't bear to lift my chin to see their faces. This wasn't the only moment in my life where I kept my eyes down.

We all leaned in.

As he wrote, I grew terrified he would ask me to speak. I have no words for my past. I only know how to speak through my body. Short phrases of breath: the rise and fall of rhythms deep within, the punctuation of my fingertips. These were my sentences.

He kept writing, I wondered if he imagined the day all our stones would disintegrate into sand. Then in a whisper he said, "Let the one who is without sin cast the first stone."

His hand still traced his thoughts in the sand.

Pressure grew. Time passed. The heat flamed through my chest, my face. I burned from head to toe, ashamed and enraged. With my eyes cast to the ground, a stone fell to my left, then to my right. Quiet thuds pulsed the sediment at our feet. When I looked around, the men were gone.

Then he spoke to me. "Woman, where are they? Has no one condemned you?"

I lifted my eyes to his face, "No one, sir." Pressure. Time. Heat. The sound of my voice cracked in disbelief.

He told me not to sin again.

I let this news settle in.

But that word he used for sin was new to my ears. Sin wasn't just breaking the law, or missing the mark, or being caught in adultery. He wanted more of me: the best of my flesh, the deepest of words. Could I tap into both? Could the sediment of my past become sentiment expressed in grace and truth? I've always used only my body to communicate. Could my own flesh become word?

I've relied all my life on the cracks and fissures of my body, that stony façade, to tell my story. Now, my voice is needed to speak this good news.

Wasn't it said of this man that even the stones would shout?

MARY MAGDALENE

Jo-Ann Badley

Although tradition has turned her into a prostitute, Mary Magdalene is never identified as such in the canonical Gospels. She is, rather, a follower and friend of Jesus, a woman whom Jesus had healed of seven demons (Luke 8:2–3), and a prominent witness at his crucifixion and burial (Matthew 27:55–61; 28:1–10). When all or most of the male disciples had scattered, she and other women remained steadfast. According to John 20:1–18, Mary Magdalene was the first disciple to whom Jesus appeared after his death.

I AM NEAR THE end of my life. And I long to see God face to face. I long to remain with God—not a visitation, but to remain.

I have not lived as other women live, and I don't expect to be remembered as other women are remembered. My story is not a typical woman's story. I have loved with my whole person—my affections and my energies—as other women have, but my loving has not looked like other women's loving. I have washed and repaired, but not at laundry stones. People ate with me and were nourished, but not only from my cooking fires. I have borne children but they came from my desire for God. They did not come from my womb but from the compassion awakened within me.

My story starts in obscurity and darkness. I was born with a deformity that marred my person, outside and in, so that I was excluded from my community. And my community was a village no one remembers once they have left it. How can you be more marginal than to be excluded from an obscure village? I would not have survived except that my father owned land, and I was the only heir. His status bought me safety. After he died, I continued in his place. But I was a marked woman in an unremarkable village, a painful combination of disfigured and lonely. I had my family's security but no family; I had independence in a world secured by ties and connections.

In retrospect, I see that *marginal* and *excluded* come with a gift. I can see things when I am not seen. If I am invisible, I can be present anywhere. I learned to make sense of the world that ignored me, to read small cues for great insights. But I would not have named *marginal* or *invisible* as a gift if I had remained diseased and lonely in that village.

One day our insignificant town received a visitation. An unusual man arrived and I was the first to meet him. But it wasn't the kind of meeting you might expect. I was certainly captivated by him, but then so was everyone else. What was he? Certainly a lover, but not with a love that begets children. A teacher? A prophet? A sage? A miracle worker? A political leader? Some of all of that but no one was really certain. Charismatic for sure.

I didn't expect him to notice me, but he did. He looked right at me, and then he reached out to touch me. I hadn't been touched for years. I drew back at first, but then I was drawn to him as if by enchanted music. I couldn't resist moving forward. He touched my face and held it gently with his hand. His thumb brushed my cheek. And with his touch, I was changed. I was transformed immediately, outside and in. I felt it. My body straightened and my mumbling stopped. The spirits that had deformed me and pushed me to the margins of my village left me. It was as though the darkness in my mind and body could not remain before the light that came from him. My internal discord was instantly ordered. I who had been deranged, who had been possessed by demons, was rearranged. I became self-possessed.

Instantly I became visible in my community. When I turned and looked at the people around me, I looked directly at them, not through them. And they looked right back at me, not past me. They did not avert their eyes. But the change to my body and my mind confused my neighbors. Now I was a regular person, but I did not have a regular place. I should have been married already, but I wasn't. I should have had children already, but I didn't. I was too old to be sought as a wife. No one knew what to do with an unattached woman recently made presentable. I was no longer unfit, but still a stranger.

I was, however, welcomed into the community of his followers. I joined the crowds whenever he was near my village. He stayed in my home and ate at my table. The reason I had been excluded from my village became the reason I was celebrated in this group. I listened to his words and was caught up with his grand vision. So much of what he said wasn't reasonable, but I loved it. My imagination and my heart were stirred. My body tingled as though I were finally fully alive.

His group of followers grew, but they certainly weren't grand: poor fishermen, a few tax collectors, lots of backwater nobodies. And always crowds who wanted food or who needed healing, as I had needed it. So many came just to hear him speak of another world, where the excluded were included, where all were healthy, where there was enough food, where there were no overlords and where everyone shared what they had. Just imagine a life like that! We all could imagine it when we listened to him. It was as though he sang an anthem from God, offering the melody for all to sing, and I gladly joined the chorus.

Eventually I left my village to join his rag tag group. It was a big step to take, but my servants could continue as they always had, and there was no particular reason to stay. His followers were mostly men and he drew some of them into an inner circle. They seemed to need teaching; they did not have the "advantage" of years of watching from the margins. Sometimes he withdrew from their needs and questions, came to me, and we would talk. I had never had anyone before with whom I shared a world. We were comfortable together. He listened to what I observed in our group. But our companionship made some of the men jealous. You might say that I was marked again, this time by resentment, and some pressed to move me to the margins. They misrepresented my past to use it against me. They insinuated that my body had been violated, not just deformed. But his respect secured my place.

Other women also joined the group—Joanna, Salome, Susanna, and the mothers of several of the men. We became friends. We talked about everything—where we had come from, what we hoped for. I had never had women friends before, certainly not anyone with whom I shared my life like this. We walked together and talked about our lives. We laughed, often at the ways some of the men misunderstood this prophet and were reprimanded by him. We slept together. It was a safe place for us. The whole group lived simply, and many people showed us hospitality because we were travelling with such a charismatic teacher. Those of us with money helped with the group's expenses, such as they were.

And his charisma passed to the rest of us. We went out in pairs to villages along the way. I took a young woman with me who had recently joined us. She had been blind and now could see. We drew small crowds because of our obvious joy, fairly dancing as we told our stories. It was as though we had learned to sing God's anthem and could now teach it to others. I touched people as I had been touched, gently yet with authority, and they too became whole. My joy increased because I could make bodies and minds healthy with just a touch! One day villagers brought a girl to me who was deformed. She reminded me of my early years and I wept. As I cried, my tears fell on her, and they healed her. It was like a birth, except she was grown, and I gave her new life, not first life.

Eventually we turned toward Jerusalem. I had never been there before. What woman goes to Jerusalem? I went to Jerusalem. The trip was exciting: maybe a hundred miles, and it took us days. We had to travel slowly on account of the many stops to attend to those who wanted to listen or be healed. It was like a little parade that went on and on. I don't know what we expected at the end, but there was euphoria all along the way. My friendship with the other women grew as we went along, but increasingly they came to me for counsel. No longer was I invisible, rather I was sought out. When I remembered my years of exclusion, I wept.

By the time we arrived in Jerusalem, we were a good-sized group and I could see immediately that our presence was annoying some of the temple leaders. They started challenging our way of life, his authority, his relationship to the Romans, almost every word and action. But our prophet didn't back down; he always had some clever retort. His responses made me laugh, but they also made me nervous. That kind of cleverness makes its own trouble.

I became uneasy about other things. There were people, not from of our group, who acted in his name. But what did he say? "Whoever is not against us is for us." I wondered if a group could survive with such open boundaries. And people who were part of our group vied for the places of honor near him. What did he say? "Whoever will be honored must be baptized as I will be baptized." I wondered how water could correct such striving for power. He spoke about suffering and death, but as though they were not the last word. I knew enough about suffering and rejection to know they were powerful forces. Was their power not final? I asked my questions but he was quiet.

So many loved him as I did. His words created hope for a better world, a fairer world, a kinder world, a world where the little people are not forgotten. And that was a place where I wanted to live. He made us think that there could be a place where steadfast love and faithfulness would meet, where righteousness and peace would kiss each other. And that was a place where I wanted to remain. I belonged there, and his initial healing touch with his continuing love for me brought me closer to that place. I was listening and learning the melody of this anthem we were singing, but I also began to hear a quiet disharmony in the background. I recognized it from my earlier years.

We reached Jerusalem at Passover. He knew of a room where we could celebrate the festival together—like a family. I planned our supper and we bought the provisions. The women cooked together and then we all ate together. It was just like the first heady days in Galilee. I sat next to him that evening and watched the feast. He spoke again of being broken and poured out, and I saw the puzzlement on the men's faces. Peter was full of bravado. Judas was disgusted. James and John simply did not understand. By the end of the meal, the discord was loud, louder than the melody, but I seemed to be the only one who feared it. I won't ever forget his pouring the cup of wine. As he did it, he looked at me as though he knew that I would understand.

It turned out my fears were justified. We knew other Jews did not like our way of life, but they didn't have enough power to act. We knew they were afraid of possible riots that would anger the Romans. But it turned out his enemies had access to the right Roman ears. And it also turned out that our "family" was made up of people you couldn't count on. Judas went to the authorities and promised to help them arrest him. I think they promised him money. What got into him? We had never been short of the things we needed. That last night, Peter denied over and over that he was one of our group. So much for bravado. The other men scattered.

And the crowds? They had been so happy to receive from him, and now they called for his death. In the end, only we women stayed close to him. I went through that night as close to him as I had been in the days in Galilee, and some of the other women stayed with me. Women do not threaten those with power—it is as if we are invisible. The Romans didn't care if a bunch of grieving women watched from the margins.

I watched the Romans crucify him. If he had been important enough, they probably would have crucified more of our group. But he was just a rabble-rouser from the backcountry, so he died alone. I had never seen a crucifixion before. It is an ugly way to die: first the beatings and mockery, then the weight of the body pulling on the arms until one can no longer breathe. His end imitated my beginning: a painful combination of disfigured and lonely. My singing and dancing went silent.

We wept through it all—women together in grief. Those were difficult hours and I re-entered the darkness. When he was dead, I watched a man who had some sway with the authorities take the body down and put it in a tomb. At least the body was not left to be consumed by the birds, as most were. I have never felt so powerless and empty in my life. My body felt hollow and my hands were numb. I couldn't touch anyone or stand to have anyone touch me.

Most of us came back together at the end of that horrible day. We straggled in alone and in small groups, but no one spoke much. The camaraderie of the road was over. How could I talk to people I didn't trust anymore? What could anyone say when our expectations had been dashed? Most of us kept silent or we wept. The ones who spoke accused others of betraying him or talked of taking up arms to avenge him. It was stupid talk, a waste of breath. We said over and over how we had hoped he was the one to redeem Israel. We said over and over how we couldn't believe that this was the way the music had ended. We endured that Sabbath. How do you celebrate the Sabbath when all hope is gone, when the community has been broken? I began to think about how I would get back to my village in Galilee. I talked to several of the women about taking spices to the tomb before we left the city. It is a woman's place to attend to the dead, and they agreed to help me.

I got up early on the first day of the week and several of us left to buy the spices we needed. I ignored the disarray of the group and found my things to walk out into the streets. My thoughts were confused because I had not planned a future and now I needed one. Whatever end I had hoped for when we left Galilee, I had not considered a funeral. Whatever else I had planned to buy, I had not thought of burial spices. As we walked, I wondered how we would get the tomb open, and if the body would already be decaying. We didn't speak much; each woman was lost in her own world. We all wanted to be in a different world, but we faithfully did what was necessary in this one.

As we came close to the tomb, we realized that someone had come before us—the tomb was open. So we ran, and we saw immediately that the body was gone. Who had stolen it? Where had it been taken? What happened next is hard to describe—in retrospect, the details of that day are a blur. The open tomb was full of light. If the grave was like a temple, it was as though the Holy of Holies had been opened to us and we saw God. The hollowness of my body was filled with light and my hands tingled. It was a second visitation. But no one sees God and lives! So perhaps it was an angel that told us to go and tell the others to wait for Jesus to come. We have talked about that day so often and we still cannot agree about the details. But I know this for certain: I went to the tomb, Jesus called me by name, and I turned and saw him. I knew it was he. When you have learned a love song by heart, you recognize it when you hear it. He spoke my name and I heard our song.

I returned to the others. I told them what I had seen and heard. Of course they didn't believe me. They demanded to know why he would come first to me. Then they went to the tomb themselves and found it empty as I had said. It was as it had been on the road. Some had new respect for me when it turned out I was right, and some had veiled resentment. Some wanted to hear the story of my exchange with him in the garden over and over again, and others wanted to silence my witness. Over the next days, he showed himself to some of the others, but they didn't recognize him. They told us later that they had walked for miles with him, talking all the while, without suspecting it was he. I wondered how they could not know his voice.

Now I had to learn how to be with him all over again. In Galilee and Jerusalem, we had walked and laughed together; we had loved each other; we had dreamed together. I had listened to him and he had listened to me. But now, things were not quite the same: he could just appear in the midst of groups as though he had been present all along; he walked through walls. I couldn't hold his hand. He couldn't touch my face. And yet things were just the same: he had wounds on his hands and feet; he ate fish. The man I knew remained with me, but he had changed. Death was not the last word. My compassion and joy, my charisma, returned. Every hollow space in my body was filled with life.

These later visitations changed me in ways no one could ever have imagined. His visit to my village, my little miracle, was nothing compared to this. Who expects a man you saw crucified to call your name, or to come and eat fish with you? But what do you do once you know someone in this way? Clearly life goes on, but it doesn't go on as a ragtag bunch in a little parade to Jerusalem—too much is different. And you don't remain in your village on your father's estate either.

I returned to my village, but I sold the estate. I began to visit other towns. I sang the anthem I had learned, both melody and harmony. I touched bodies and minds to make them whole. I baptized, and I offered bread and wine in memory of him. My life was poured out to birth and mother communities who learned from me the word of new life. I healed and loved because I had been healed and loved. I listened and spoke wisdom because I had been seen and heard. I bore witness to the changes that are possible because I was loved.

Now I am far from where I started in my father's village. The end of my life is near. This is certainly not how I expected my life to end. But I am at home among those who love me; their love celebrates my beauty. They are grateful for my wisdom and my touch. I know others are still jealous of me. And I know my story is confused with other women's stories—as though all women's stories are the same! The jealousy and confusion render me invisible and marginal among some. They smear my name. But among those who love me I am respected and sought out. I am at home. Almost. I still wait for God's visitation, to be touched and drawn in further, to join in the great alleluia of God's eternal anthem.

PRISCA

Maggie Watters

In three letters, Paul includes greetings from the couple Prisca and Aquila, and claims that they are fellow workers with him, that a church met in their house, and that they had risked their life for his sake (1 Corinthians 16:19; Romans 16:3; 2 Timothy 4:19). In Acts 18, Luke says that Paul stayed in the house of Priscilla (a diminutive form of Prisca) and Aquila in Corinth, joined them in tent making, and later established the couple in Ephesus. Biblical scholars suggest that, because Prisca's name precedes Aquila's in several references, she was the more influential or memorable partner. A few even argue that she was the author of the New Testament epistle to the Hebrews. But, troubled by the presence of a strong woman in the church, some early biblical translators reversed the order of their names, or "unnamed" her altogether as merely "Aquila's wife," such that she is often forgotten.

Do you know who I am? You should. You all should. I'm not like the others and I never have been. Yet how is it that I've been thrown into this faction with the rest of them, the women who can't speak or stand up for themselves? Know who I am.

Move? We had been stripped of our home and of our livelihood; we had no choice. We knew a time would come when we would be thrown out of Rome by our ever-charming emperor, Claudius. God, grant me serenity! It isn't fair! I guess we are lucky that our tent-making business travels so well and can be set up just about anywhere. But, where are all of these people going to meet for worship, if not at my house? Do you know who I am?

Upon moving to Corinth, I again established a place where people could come to worship and be taught the Word of God. Did you not recognize me as you walked through the door of my home, the home I so graciously gave as a sacred place? Do you think I'm being arrogant, only gloating of my prosperity? Maybe opening my home and serving, like a good disciple should, was the only way I could get you to listen, as I have every right to speak when the Holy Spirit speaks to me. My home was the place where you were hungry and filled, the place where you could feel safe, the place where you worshiped. I worked tirelessly building it, but gave it all to the Lord. Do you know who I am?

I am the one who provided nourishment for the souls of others as I stood before you and spoke of a God that would deliver us all. Know who I am. Know that Apostle Paul found me by the hand of God and that, as a teacher myself, I influenced Paul's teachings for the better, benefiting the church community. In turn he taught me more about his own understandings. Know that I put my life on the line for Paul, looking for no reward. Know that because of me Apollos is able to effectively spread the Word by his elegant speeches like the one heard outside of the temple. I am an authoritative teacher and trainer. Still you ask who I am?

I refuse to be kept silent. I am a preacher, teacher, and patron of other believers. I am respected for my hard work. When some Hebrew members of our community suffered persecution and decided to give up and go back to the synagogue, I risked everything to write a letter to convince them that Jesus offered them far more than the temple religion ever could. Many of them came back, and they kept my letter, although later they erased my name from the last page of the epistle. No wonder you do not know who I am.

Even when Paul left, I continued to keep the house church going; I preached to the people, fed them. I was able to continue the work because I am not alone. Aquila—he is my partner, my helper, my other half, my equal. Of course he knows me. Always at my side, we generate an inimitable energy, a passion that cannot be subdued. Once upon a time he knew me bodily; he knew me deeply. Intimately and gently. Perfectly intertwined, we became one. But desperate times call for desperate measures! I came to realize that time spent in love and ecstasy was energy that we could be spending adoring the Lord, in work, in spreading the good news until Jesus returned. I didn't want to risk the burdens of motherhood, inevitable for me if we had kept carrying on as we were. "Do not deprive each other except by mutual consent," my dear friend argued when I told him. But in the end, Aquila regarded my words and saw that I was right. We desire God's eternal Word more than fleeting pleasures of the flesh. We labor hard for our business, and we strive to provide a comfortable environment for our many guests. We share the wealth God has given us with other apostles. Sometimes desire overtakes us and we stumble into each other's arms. But in doing the work God has given us, we come together to fortify our love by the Holy Spirit. He knows me. Do you?

Sisters, you should know me! Why do you resign yourselves to being meek while I toil for your liberation, toil constantly by the side of them, your oppressors? Why do you not defend yourselves, your sisters, from the humiliation you have suffered at their hands? Why let them have dominion over the world that is just as much yours as theirs? You owe them respect, but do they owe you nothing? They feel dominant only because you let them. Is this your way of shirking responsibility? How far you are from the reign of God!

Brothers, is it simply that women have gotten used to this position where they obey you—you, their husbands, brothers, even strange men on the street? Or must you work hard to keep them down? Either way, it is time that you stopped. Do I scare you? Am I too much woman? Perhaps you should be afraid. I have been more important in the church—more of a church father—than you'll ever be. I have instructed apostles. I have spoken for Jesus. I have offered my home for a church, my body as a living sacrifice, and my life as a servant of God. I have left my words in your Bible. I am standing up for those who can't, and I am speaking for those who are silent. I am Prisca.

Do you now know who I am?

QUESTIONS FOR DISCUSSION

1. How familiar are you with the Bible? Were any of these stories unfamiliar to you? Which one(s) surprised you the most, and why?

2. How familiar are you with *The Vagina Monologues*? If you have seen (or read) the play, what did you think of it? If you haven't seen it, what do you imagine it is about? Did this volume confirm or change your thoughts about the play?

3. See a production or read the script of *The Vagina Monologues*. (It is often performed on college campuses in the month of February or March). Identify some of the features of these monologues. What is gained when women tell the stories of their bodies? What is lost?

4. What do you think of the editors' choice to combine biblical stories with narratives about women's bodies, through the lens of *The Vagina Monologues*? What do you think is gained by such a move? What is lost?

5. What are some of the positive and negative effects of reading the Bible through the monologues in this volume, as written by authors from several different stages and walks of life?

6. Some of the monologues use language that stays closer to the biblical language or to traditional literary forms; others incorporate more contemporary syntax, sometimes even including profanity. What difference do the authors' language choices make for how you read them?

7. In these monologues, the women telling their stories face various challenges. Often, these challenges are men, but sometimes they are also economic oppression, social ideas about gender roles, health issues, God, or even other women. With relation to the challenges they faced, which of the narrators invoked the greatest sympathy in you?

8. These monologues reflect a wide variety of theological beliefs and assumptions. Which one(s) most closely coincide with your own theology? Which ones challenge you the most? Were these challenges empowering or simply disturbing?

9. Identify some of the ways that both women and men talk today about women's bodies in public. What influences the ways that female bodies are described? Do you think that these types of descriptions promote or inhibit healthy attitudes toward female bodies?

10. What taboos are there in discussing women's bodies? What is the purpose of these taboos? Are they healthy or problematic, or possibly both?

11. Before reading one of the monologues in this book, read the biblical account (references are provided in the introduction to each story). Imagine how you might tell this story from the perspective of the woman's body. Then read the monologue. How is it different than your version? What is missing? What is added? Consider how your personal experience affects the telling of these stories. Is one version more "true" than another?

12. Write your own "vagina monologue." Consider performing it. What emotions rise up for you? What kinds of responses do you think you would get, and how much does that depend on who the audience is?

13. For each of these monologues, identify the "women's issue" at stake. Do some research on the web to find out how prevalent this issue is in your own neighborhood, region, and/or

globally. How does the monologue affect your understanding of this issue?

14. To what public conversations about current events (such as health care, reproduction, economic equality, the definition of marriage, parenthood, war, etc.) do you think this volume most helpfully contributes? Why?

15. Look up the biblical references to these stories in a traditional Bible commentary. What does it focus on? What does it say about these women? Compare several commentaries. How are commentaries similar to or different from the monologues? Compare regular commentaries with some of the books in the bibliography below.

16. In what ways, if any, do these monologues challenge your thinking about the role of women in faith communities? What actions will you take as a result?

17. In what ways, if any, do these monologues challenge your thinking about the bodies of other women and girls, both people you know personally and people you will never meet? What actions will you take as a result?

18. In what ways, if any, do these monologues challenge your thinking about your own body? What actions will you take as a result?

19. This collection merely scratches the surface of all the biblical stories that include women. There are countless others who didn't make it into these pages. Which monologues do you wish were in the volume? If you were going to write your own biblical monologue, which character would you choose and why?

20. The editors write, "Our hope is to open the biblical texts, to read them in new ways, to become more aware of the complex relationships of power and gender that existed then and exist now, and thus to promote a dominant ethic of compassionate listening." Did this volume accomplish its stated task? Why or why not?

BIBLIOGRAPHY

Ackerman, Susan. *Warrior, Dancer, Seductress, Queen: Women in Judges and Biblical Israel*. New York: Doubleday, 1998.

Adelman, Penina. "Hannah." In *Praise Her Works: Conversations with Biblical Women*, edited by P. Adelman, 67–74. Philadelphia: Jewish Publication Society, 2005.

Bach, Alice, editor. *Women in the Hebrew Bible: A Reader*. New York: Routledge, 1999.

Bal, Mieke. *Murder and Difference: Gender, Genre, and Scholarship on Sisera's Death*. Bloomington: Indiana University Press, 1988.

Beach, Eleanor Ferris. *The Jezebel Letters: Religion and Politics in Ninth-Century Israel*. Minneapolis: Fortress, 2005.

Bellis, Alice Ogden. *Helpmates, Harlots, and Heroes: Women's Stories in the Hebrew Bible*. Louisville: Westminster John Knox, 1994, 2007.

Berquist, Jon L. *Reclaiming Her Story: The Witness of Women in the Old Testament*. St. Louis: Chalice, 1992.

Blanchard, Kathryn D. "Who's Afraid of *The Vagina Monologues*?: Christian Responses and Responsibility to Women on Campus and in the Global Community." *Journal of the Society of Christian Ethics* 30/2 (2010) 99–122.

Brenner, Athalya. *I Am . . . : Biblical Women Tell Their Own Stories*. Minneapolis: Fortress, 2005.

———. *Judges*. Feminist Companion to the Bible, 2nd ser., 4. New York: Sheffield Academic, 1999.

Brooten, Bernadette J. "Paul's Views on the Nature of Women and Female Homoeroticism." In *Immaculate and Powerful: The Female in Sacred Image and Social Reality*, edited by Clarissa Atkinson, Constance Buchanan, and Margaret R. Miles, 61–87. Boston: Beacon, 1985.

Boullogne, Louis de. *Christ and the Woman Subject to Bleeding*. Beaux Arts Museum, Renees, France.

Carmody, Denise Lardner. *Biblical Woman: Contemporary Reflections on Scriptural Texts*. New York: Crossroad, 1988.

Caveny, Kathleen. "Be Not Afraid: 'The Vagina Monologues' on Catholic Campuses," *Commonweal*, March 13, 2009, 16–22.

Bibliography

Christ, Carol P. "Expressing Anger at God." In *Women's Studies in Religion: A Multicultural Reader*, edited by Kate Bagley and Kathleen McIntosh. Upper Saddle River, NJ: Pearson/Prentice Hall, 2007.

Daly, Mary. "The Women's Movement: An Exodus Community." *Religious Education* 67 (1972) 327–33.

Dennis, Trevor. *Sarah Laughed: Women's Voices in the Old Testament*. Nashville: Abingdon, 1994.

Diski, Jenny. *Only Human: A Divine Comedy*. New York: Picador, 2002.

Dube, Musa W. "Fifty Years of Bleeding: A Storytelling Feminist Reading of Mark 5:24–43." In *Other Ways of Reading: African Women and the Bible*, edited by Musa W. Dube, 50–60. Atlanta: Society of Biblical Literature, 2001.

Dutcher-Walls, Patricia. *Jezebel: Portraits of a Queen*. Collegeville: Liturgical, 1989.

Ellis, Elizabeth. "Justa the Canaanite Woman." In Volume 13 of *The Storyteller's Companion to the Bible*, edited by D. Smith and M. Williams, 72–78. Nashville: Abingdon, 1999.

Ensler, Eve. *The Vagina Monologues: The V-Day Edition*. New York: Villard, 2001, 2007.

———. *The Vagina Monologues: The Official Script for the 2010 V-Day Campaigns*. New York: Dramatists Play Service, 2009.

———. *The Vagina Monologues*, tenth anniversary edition. New York: Villard, 2008.

———, and Joyce Tenneson. *Vagina Warriors*. New York: Bulfinch, 2005.

Fewell, Danna Nolan, and David M. Gunn. "Controlling Perspectives: Women, Men, and the Authority of Violence in Judges 4–5." *Journal of the American Academy of Religion* 58/3 (1990) 389–411.

Garland, David E. *Reading Matthew: A Literary and Theological Commentary on the First Gospel*. New York: Crossroad, 1995.

Garland, Diana R., and David E. Garland. *Flawed Families of the Bible: How God's Grace Works through Imperfect Relationships*. Grand Rapids: Brazos, 2007.

Gartner, Rosanne. *Meet Bathsheba: Dramatic Portraits of Biblical Women*. Valley Forge, PA: Judson, 2000.

Gench, Frances Taylor. *Back to the Well: Women's Encounters with Jesus in the Gospels*. Louisville: Westminster John Knox, 2004.

Gettleman, Jeffrey. "Fighting Congo's Ills with Education and an Army of Women." *New York Times*, February 6, 2011, 6.

Graetz, Naomi. *S/He Created Them: Feminist Retellings of Biblical Stories*. Piscataway, NJ: Gorgias, 2003.

Gravett, Sandie. "Reading 'Rape' in the Hebrew Bible: A Consideration of Language." *Journal for the Study of the Old Testament* 28/3 (2004): 279–299.

Guest, Deryn. *When Deborah Met Jael: Lesbian Biblical Hermeneutics*. New York: SCM, 2005.

Hackett, Jo A. "1 and 2 Samuel." In *Women's Bible Commentary*, edited by Carol A. Newsom and Sharon H. Ringe, 91–100. Expanded ed. Louisville: Westminster John Knox, 1998.

———. "In the Days of Jael: Reclaiming the History of Women in Ancient Israel." In *Immaculate and Powerful: The Female in Sacred Image and Social Reality*, edited by Clarissa Atkinson, Constance Buchanan, and Margaret R. Miles, 15–38. Boston: Beacon, 1985.

———. "Violence and Women's Lives in the Book of Judges." *Interpretation* 58/4 (2004) 356–64.

Hammer, Jill. *Sisters at Sinai: New Tales of Biblical Women*. Philadelphia: Jewish Publication Society, 2001.

Hammer, Reuven. *The Classic Midrash: Tannaitic Commentaries on the Bible*. New York: Paulist, 1995.

Harrington, Daniel J. *Interpreting the Old Testament: A Practical Guide*. Collegeville, MN: Liturgical, 1981.

Heine, Susanne. *Women in Early Christianity: A Reappraisal*. Translated by John Bowden. Minneapolis: Augsburg, 1988.

Henderson, Lois T. *Lydia: A Novel*. San Francisco: Harper and Row, 1979.

———, with Harold Ivan Smith, *Priscilla and Aquila: A Novel*. San Francisco: Harper and Row, 1985.

Higgs, Liz Curtis. *Bad Girls of the Bible and What We Can Learn from Them*. Colorado Springs, CO: Waterbrook, 1999.

———. *Really Bad Girls of the Bible: More Lessons from Less-than-Perfect Women*. Colorado Springs, CO: Waterbrook, 2000.

———. *Slightly Bad Girls of the Bible: Flawed Women Loved by a Flawless God*. Colorado Springs, CO: Waterbrook, 2007.

———. *Unveiling Mary Magdalene: Discovering the Truth about a Not-So-Bad-Girl of the Bible*. Colorado Springs, CO: Waterbrook, 2004.

Huber, Lynn R., Dan W. Clanton Jr., and Jane S. Webster. "Biblical Subjects in Art." In *Teaching the Bible Through Popular Culture and the Arts*, edited by Mark Roncase and Patrick Gray, 197–228. Atlanta: Society of Biblical Literature, 2007.

Jacobs, Harriet. *Incidents in the Life of a Slave Girl*. New York: Oxford, 1988.

Kugel, James L. *The Bible as It Was*. Cambridge, MA: Harvard University Press, 1997.

Lancaster, Sarah Hearner. *Women and the Authority of Scripture: A Narrative Approach*. Harrisburg, PA: Trinity, 2002.

L'Engle, Madeleine. *Walking on Water: Reflections on Faith and Art*. Wheaton, IL: Harold Shaw, 1980.

Lerner, Harriet. "V Is for Vulva, Not Just Vagina." *Lawrence Journal-World and News*. May 4, 2003. Online: http://www2.ljworld.com/news/2003/may/04/v_is_for.

Levine, Amy-Jill. "Matthew." In *Women's Bible Commentary*, edited by Carol A. Newsome and Sharon H. Ringe, 339–49. Expanded ed. Louisville: Westminster John Knox, 1998.

Bibliography

————, editor. *A Feminist Companion to John*. Vol. 2. Feminist Companion to the New Testament and Early Christian Writings 5. New York: Sheffield Academic, 2003.

Mayeski, Marie Anne. "'Let Women Not Despair': Rabanus Maurus on Women as Prophets." *Theological Studies* 58/2 (1997) 237–53.

McCarter, P. Kyle. "1 Samuel: Introduction and Notes." In *The HarperCollins Study Bible: Including Apocryphal and Deutercanonical Books*, Harold W. Attridge, general editor, 389–434. Student ed.; rev. ed. San Francisco: HarperSanFrancisco, 2006.

McKenna, Megan. *Not Counting Women and Children: Neglected Stories from the Bible*. Maryknoll, NY: Orbis, 1994.

Meehan, Bridget Mary. *Praying With Women of the Bible*. Liguori, MO: Liguori/ Triumph, 1998.

Meyers, Carol, editor. *Women in Scripture*. Grand Rapids: Eerdmans, 2000.

Miller, Casey, and Kate Swift. "Desexing the Language." *MS*, December 1971.

————. *The Handbook of Nonsexist Writing: For Writers, Editors, and Speakers*. 2nd ed. Bloomington, IN: iUniverse, 2001.

————. *Words and Women*. New York: Doubleday, 1976.

Miller, Wiley. *Non Sequitur*, April 8, 2012. Online: htttp://www.gocomics.com/ nonsequitur/2012/04/08.

Murphy, Cullen. *The Word According to Eve: Women and the Bible in Ancient Times and Our Own*. Boston: Houghton Mifflin, 1998.

Neusner, Jacob. *The Midrash: An Introduction*. Northvale, NJ: J. Aronson, 1990.

Niditch, Susan. "Eroticism and Death in the Tale of Jael." In *Women in the Hebrew Bible: A Reader*, edited by Alice Bach, 305–15. New York: Routledge, 1999.

Nunally-Cox, Janice. *Fore-Mothers: Women of the Bible*. New York: Seabury, 1981.

Osbeck, Kenneth W. *52 Bible Characters Dramatized: Easy-to-Use Monologues for All Occasions*. Grand Rapids: Kregel, 1996.

Ostriker, Alicia Suskin. *Feminist Revision and the Bible*. Cambridge, MA: Blackwell, 1993.

————. *For the Love of God: The Bible as an Open Book*. New Brunswick, NJ: Rutgers, 2007.

Pardes, Ilana. *Countertraditions in the Bible: A Feminist Approach*. Cambridge: Harvard University Press, 1992.

Reger, Jo, and Lacey Story. "Talking About My Vagina: Two College Campuses and *The Vagina Monologues*." In *Different Wavelengths: Studies of the Contemporary Women's Movement*, edited by Jo Reger, 154–55. New York: Routledge, 2005.

Rosen, Norma Gangel. *Biblical Women Unbound: Counter-Tales*. Philadelphia: Jewish Publication Society, 1996.

Schaberg, Jane. *The Resurrection of Mary Magdalene*. New York: Continuum, 2004.

Scham, Sandra. "The Days of the Judges: When Men and Women Were Animals and Trees Were Kings." *Journal for the Study of the Old Testament* 97 (2002) 37–64.

Scholz, Susanne, *Sacred Witness: Rape in the Hebrew Bible*. Minneapolis: Fortress, 2010.

Schüssler Fiorenza, Elisabeth. *Bread Not Stone: The Challenge of Feminist Biblical Interpretation*. Boston: Beacon, 1984.

——. *In Memory of Her: A Feminist Theological Reconstruction of Christian Origins*. New York: Crossroad, 1992.

——. "Feminist Hermeneutics." in Volume II of *Anchor Bible Commentary*, David Noel Freedman, general editor, 783–791. New York: Doubleday, 1992.

——. *In Searching the Scriptures: A Feminist Commentary*. New York: Crossroad, 1994.

Shepherd, Kate. "Mandatory Transvaginal Ultrasounds: Coming Soon to a State near You." *Mother Jones*, March 5, 2012. Online: http://www.motherjones .com/mojo/2012/03/transvaginal-ultrasounds-coming-soon-state-near-you.

Spiner, Trent. "Police: Girl raped, then relocated." *Concord Monitor*, May 25, 2010. Online: http://www.concordmonitor.com/article/police-girl-raped-then -relocated?page=0%2C1.

Sprague, William B., editor. *Women of the Old and New Testaments*. New York: D. Appleton, 1849.

Taylor, J. Glen. "The Song of Deborah and Two Canaanite Goddesses." *Journal for the Study of the Old Testament* 23 (1982) 99–108.

Teubal, Savina J. *Hagar the Egyptian*. New York: Harper and Row, 1990.

Torbett, David. "'I Did Not Wash My Feet with That Woman': Using Dramatic Performance to Teach Biblical Studies." *Teaching Theology and Religion* 13/4 (2010) 307–19.

Trible, Phyllis. *Texts of Terror*. Philadelphia: Fortress, 1984.

——, and Letty M. Russell, editors. *Hagar, Sarah, and Their Children: Jewish, Christian, and Muslim Perspectives*. Louisville: Westminster John Knox, 2006.

Van Wijk-Bos, Johanna W. H. "Out of the Shadows: Genesis 38; Judges 4:17–22; Ruth 3." *Semeia* 42 (1988) 37–67.

"V-Day Statement in Response to the Cardinal Newman Society's Attempt to Ban V-Day Benefit Productions of 'The Vagina Monologues.'" Online: http://www.vday.org/node/1464.

Vincent, Mark A. "The Song of Deborah: A Structural and Literary Consideration." *Journal for the Study of the Old Testament* 91 (2000) 61–82.

Viner, Katharine. "Top 100 Women: Eve Ensler." *The Guardian*, March 8, 2011. Online: http://www.guardian.co.uk/books/2011/mar/08/eve-ensler-100-women.

Walker, Barbara G. *Women's Rituals: A Sourcebook*. New York: HarperCollins, 1990.

Whitley, Katerina Katsarka. *Speaking for Ourselves: Voices of Biblical Women*. Harrisburg, PA: Morehouse, 1998.

Bibliography

Williams, Mary Elizabeth. "Television's Season of the Vagina." In Salon. September 26, 2011. Online: www.salon.com/2011/09/26/vagina_sitcom_season.

Williams, Michael E. "Judith." In vol. 4 of *The Storyteller's Companion to the Bible*, edited by Michael E. Williams, 187–93. Nashville: Abingdon, 1993.

Wolf, Naomi. *Vagina: A New Biography*. New York: Ecco, 2012.

Yeats, William Butler. "Leda and the Swan." 1924. Online: http://www.poets.org/viewmedia.php/prmMID/15525.

Yee, Gale A. "By the Hand of a Woman: The Metaphor of the Woman Warrior in Judges 4." *Semeia* 61 (1993) 99–132.

———. *Poor Banished Children of Eve: Woman as Evil in the Hebrew Bible*. Minneapolis: Fortress, 2003.